FIRST

FLIGHTS

iUniverse, Inc.

New York   Bloomington

First Flights

Stories to Inspire
From Those Who Fly

Stories Collected by:
Jill Rutan Hoffman

Edited by:
Jennifer Dumke
Julie Lindell

Cover Art by:
Mark Pestana

First Flights
Stories to Inspire From Those Who Fly

iUniverse books may be ordered through booksellers or by contacting:

*iUniverse
1663 Liberty Drive
Bloomington, IN 47403
www.iuniverse.com
1-800-Authors (1-800-288-4677)*

*ISBN: 978-1-4401-3288-9 (pbk)
ISBN: 978-1-4401-3289-6 (ebk)*

Printed in the United States of America

iUniverse Rev. 06/10/2009

To the people who fly, especially my husband,
thank you for your inspiration.

I Am Solo Now
Sterling Price

I am solo now
Alone in the sky
Upon newborn wings
I can fly!

Leaving the world
Below and behind
Here with birds
What shall I find?

Caution on the airspeed
Check reference to the ground
Is the engine running
smoothly?
Is it time to turn around?

Onward!

To the heavens
My engine takes me
With new perspectives
My eyes now see

I have slipped the bonds
Where gravity reigns
Free of earth
Aloft in my plane

Correct the power setting
Does the tower know my plans?
Will this be a touch and go
Or should I just land?

Approaching base turn
Have I pulled carb heat out?
Will I make a smooth landing?
Is there any doubt?

Set flaps at seventy
Trim for sixty-five
How quick it is over
I survived!

I have soloed now
Met the challenge of the sky
With newfound courage

I will return again to fly!

CONTENTS

BEING THE FIRST

EPILOGUE

Acknowledgements

My dream of sharing these inspiring stories would not have become reality without the help of many people.

First, my most sincere gratitude goes to the authors who donated their stories to this project. Thank you for taking the time to share your personal aviation and spaceflight "firsts." You have inspired me, and you will inspire generations to come with your extraordinary tales.

Thank you to my editors Jennifer Dumke and Julie Lindell who spent many hours focused on the very delicate job of editing the wonderful stories in this book. It was very important to me not to jeopardize the purity of the authors' personal stories. Thank you Jennifer and Julie for the many hours you donated working with the technical yet delicate part of the writing process.

Next I would like to extend a special thank you to Mark Pestana. When Mark is not flying for NASA, he is spending time with his family and enjoying his passion for painting. Mark penned a fascinating story for this collection and painted the artwork that is the cover of this book. To Mark and his beautiful family, thank you for your friendship and your breathtaking painting. I shall treasure it for a lifetime.

Thank you to my beautiful daughter, Noelle, for transforming Mark's painting into a photograph. Your eye for photography allowed Mark's beautiful artwork to appear on the cover with the same vividness as the original. Also thank you for making me feel like a supermodel when taking my picture for the back cover. You are a true professional and I look forward to your great success in the world of photography.

This would not be complete without thanking my youngest daughter, Haley. Thank you for the daily sunshine you bring to my life. You are a joy and were a necessity on those days when I lost my sense of humor. Thank you for being there to help me smile again.

To Dave English, author of *Slipping the Surly Bonds* and *The Air Up There,* thank you for sharing your collection of "great aviation quotes."

A project like this book requires financial "fuel" to get it off the ground. I would like to thank Art and Geri Staden, John and Sally Hoffman, and Nell Rutan, for their early financial support to this most worthy endeavor.

The Experimental Aircraft Association has been like a family to me. I've grown up with EAA and counted the days until Oshkosh with the same anticipation other kids have for Christmas. Thank you for the constant support of my endeavors and a lifetime of memories.

Finally, I would like to thank my husband, Lars. My love for you can hardly be expressed in words. Thank you for your constant love, guidance, and support. I'm extremely lucky to have you in my life. None of the things I truly hold dear in my life, including this book, would have been possible without you. I look forward to our future adventures.

Introduction

When you hear a pilot begin a story that starts out with "There I was …" you know you're about to hear how the self proclaimed "World's Greatest Aviator" defied the odds once again. I grew up around pilots and they *love* to share their stories, complete with flying hands and sound effects. Year after year at the Oshkosh Fly-In, or as it is known today AirVenture Oshkosh, my father tells the story of how, in 1986, he set nine world and absolute aviation records by flying around the world without stopping or refueling in the flying fuel tank known as the Voyager. I've listened to that same story for over twenty years and I still sit there hanging on every word wondering if he makes it home alive. A good story can make you feel as if you are reliving the experience. You can smell the air and feel the emotions of joy, fear, excitement, and sometimes sorrow just as if you were there yourself. This book is full of such stories.

As you read through the pages of *First Flights* you'll be transported to space as you dock with the Mir Space Station, you'll float around the world in the *Breitling Orbiter 3* balloon, you'll race to the edge of our atmosphere in the X-15, and you'll experience the thrill of taking that first cross-country flight through the eyes of an apprentice pilot. These true stories, written by the pilots themselves, will have you wondering how they found enough courage to "go where they had never gone before." My hope is that these stories will inspire you and future generations to live and share their own inspiring "firsts."

I chose to fill this book with "first flight" stories because they embody the spirit of flight. Whether you're a student pilot making your first solo flight or an experienced pilot trying out a new airplane, any new experience while floating above the earth is life-changing. Amelia Earhart said, "You haven't seen a tree until you've seen its shadow from the sky." I couldn't agree more! Nothing gives you that "sitting on top of the world" feeling like expanding your personal envelope. My own first flight experience is something I will never forget.

I had completed ground school in 1995 and was eager to start flight training. My father was kind enough to offer up his expertise, along with his Cessna 150, to help me complete my training. The only problem was that I lived on the other side of the country at the time. I was finally able to add a week to the end of a business trip to California and thought that it should be possible to get through my solo flight during that week of focused flying training. In my mind all I had to do was circle the small Mojave airport a few times. How hard could that be? Besides, I grew up at that same Mojave Airport, watching my family build and fly "homebuilt" aircraft and I had flown as a passenger many times. I soon found out how different it is when you are the pilot at the controls. Dad was not thrilled with my casual attitude about flying and he made sure it was the most challenging week of my life.

At the end of my aviation "hell week," after trying to quit twice, I soloed. It was one of the most exhilarating experiences of my life. My father, who doesn't even let me drive his car, allowed me to fly his plane, alone, around that small Mojave airport. I was scared, but I was also proud of myself for having the courage to try. After a few verses of *I Am Woman* I landed that Cessna 150 and became a very serious pilot, with my own "There I was ..." story to tell.

I am now one of many who have been privileged to take their first step into the very exciting world of flight. I am also privileged to share with you, through this book, many more exciting aviation stories in the hope that they will inspire you and others to explore new worlds. Many happy landings!

Jill Rutan Hoffman

I MUST FLY

The exhilaration of flying is too keen, the pleasure too great,
for it to be neglected as a sport.
— *Orville Wright*

More than anything else the sensation is one of perfect peace
mingled with an excitement that strains every nerve to the utmost,
if you can conceive of such a combination.
— *Wilbur Wright*

Becoming Dick Rutan
Dick Rutan

A youngster—just a handful of years old—woke up all excited one morning. For today his mother was going to take him for his very first airplane ride. In the late 1940s, the Flabob Airfield in Riverside, California, was not much more than a cow pasture.

The Piper J-5 Cub was standing at the ready. It was a small, three-place airplane, with the backseat widened so that two bodies could just barely squeeze in. The airplane was in dire need of a little TLC. The paint had chipped in areas, and the stuffing was bulging from the worn seats. But today, this was the most beautiful airplane in the world.

The youngster quickly discovered that, while seated, he would not be able to see out of the window. He begged his mother to let him stand behind the pilot. He held onto the pilot's tattered backrest, hugging it so tightly that he released years of musty odor from the stuffing. The pilot started the engine and turned the tiny plane into the wind. With a huge roar and vibration, it bounced out across the field and slipped into the air.

The wide-eyed child was instantly enamored with the view of Mother Earth from his stance. He hardly took the time to blink, not wanting to miss a thing. And this moment, free as a bird and with a view he'd never forget, changed this child's life forever. The feeling of being aloft, supported only by an invisible blast of air, permeated the child's very soul and would occupy virtually every action of his life from this day forward.

This same child built runways in his backyard, beckoning airplanes to land. They never did, so he went to the airplanes. On his 16th birthday, before going for his driver's license, he went to the airport and soloed in an airplane. A couple of years later, he enlisted in the Air Force and became a fighter pilot with many great and heroic achievements. His greatest achievement, however, happened four decades after that first ride in the Piper Cub. This child, this pilot, this highly decorated, retired Lieutenant Colonel, would fly the first non-stop, unrefueled flight around the world.

No one could even imagine in the late 1940s that pilots could control a flying machine capable of flying non-stop and unrefueled around the world. The spark ignited on that chilly morning would kindle into a dream that would lead to aviation's last great "first."

Life is an adventure, and you are limited only by what you can dream.

Many First Flights
William B. Scott

Every pilot has a first-flight story, but I may be in a minority who can claim multiple "First Flights." Oh, sure, there are test pilots who can rightfully claim to have made many inaugural flights of new aircraft, but I'm talking about the first flight of a person's airborne career. How many can say they logged more than one actual "first flight?"

I can. In fact, I've logged five of them … sort of. And, somewhere, I have a different logbook to prove each one.

First as a financially challenged college student, then as a lowly paid, almost-broke Air Force one-stripe airman who dearly wanted to be a pilot, I found a system that would get me into the air at minimal cost. For $5 and the price of one *Flying Magazine*, I could get about an hour of flight training.

In the late 1960s, Cessna launched a program aimed at getting more Americans into light airplanes. If more people became pilots, Cessna would eventually sell more airplanes—at least that was their thinking. Consequently, the company's ads in magazines such as *Flying* included clip-out coupons that, when accompanied by a $5 bill, would give the bearer an introductory lesson in a Cessna 150. Being fairly adept with scissors, I managed to log five "introductory" $5 flights at different dealers/flight schools before I could finally afford to join an Air Force flying club and get serious about earning that wonderful private pilot certificate.

By my fifth (and final) "introductory" ride, I had the program pretty much figured out. I could taxi, take off, climb, and turn with some rudimentary skill. At one point, the instructor/demo pilot looked over and said, "You have an incredibly natural talent. You really should be a pilot!" I thanked him and replied that I really enjoyed flying, but was making a grand total of $70 per month at the time—as an airman in Uncle Sam's Air Force—and couldn't afford to take lessons. He said nothing, just continued to direct me through the various maneuvers, obviously impressed by this first-timer's God-given abilities, I thought smugly. My landing required his assistance on the controls, since I'd had very few chances to work on those techniques.

We taxied back to the ramp, parked, tied-down the Cessna, and walked into the building in near-silence. After signing a brand-new, giveaway logbook, the instructor looked me squarely in the eye and asked, "How many of these 'introductory' rides have you had?"

Oops. I swallowed hard and confessed to five. But before I could apologize, he laughed, slapped me on the back, and said, "If you want to fly that much, you'll find a way!" Thank you, thank you! For a moment there, I thought I was going to jail.

That was about 2,000 hours and 53 different aircraft types ago. My logbook contains everything from Cessna 150s and Piper Warriors to F-14, F-15, F-16, and F-18 fighters, the B-2 bomber simulator, and Burt Rutan's one-of-a-kind "Grizzly." It wasn't easy squeezing lessons in between a hectic work schedule and family obligations, but the GI Bill helped me eventually obtain a commercial pilot's ticket with instrument and multi-engine ratings. The Air Force sent me back to college for an electrical engineering degree; then commissioned me as a United States Air Force officer. I ultimately graduated from the Air Force Test Pilot School as a flight test engineer (FTE). My eyesight would never meet military pilot standards, so I wore contact lenses and settled for the second-best job in the Air Force—being an FTE and riding one seat behind the *best* job, that of a test pilot.

In 12 years of military and civil flight-testing and another 17 years of evaluating airplanes, helicopters, sailplanes, gyroplanes and other flying machines for *Aviation Week & Space Technology* magazine, I've logged dozens of first flights—but none as shady as the first five.

I'm still embarrassed about those "introductory" flights, but I'd like to think I've since returned far more to the industry than I took. Cessna, I extend my sincere apologies. But please accept my profuse thanks for getting this airman started. In my case, I firmly believe your program succeeded far better than you could ever have imagined.

A Gift for My Son
Kathy Serrano

In 1990, my son's upcoming college graduation loomed heavily in the forefront of my mind. He was graduating with a degree in airway science, and I wanted to give him the perfect gift for the occasion. I needed something meaningful that he would never forget. I asked a pilot, and he suggested that I learn to fly and take my son "around the patch" for his gift. I laughed! How could a charter member of "White-Knuckled Flyers" learn to fly? However, the seed of the suggestion flirted with my imagination. Me, learn to fly? No way ... well, maybe.

I contacted a pilot who put me in touch with his friends. In a joint effort, they all agreed to help alleviate my fear by taking me flying. After hours in the air, their patient efforts finally paid off. I'd finally ride with them, even if the air were a bit rough. I also came to realize that the plane would not fall from the sky. The next big step was ground school.

As a teacher, I've taken many classes, yet none had challenged me as much as ground school. I can't count the number of times I came home discouraged, crying, and ready to quit because I knew that weight and balance and VORs were concepts I could never master. But, after taking the Private Pilot Exam, I discovered that I had passed. I was thrilled, except I knew the hardest part was yet to come.

After some friendly prodding and lots of encouragement, I went on an introductory flight to see if there was a CFI (certified flight instructor) willing to take on the challenge of teaching a white-knuckled flyer to fly. After a safe landing, my instructor encouraged me to take lessons and introduced me to an older flight instructor. I will always be grateful to this very patient, understanding CFI.

9

He hardly ever acted as though he wished he had strapped on his parachute before strapping into his seatbelt.

On March 19, 1990, I soloed. All of the FBO (fixed base operators) instructors said that they had never seen anyone's knees knock the way mine had. I had an overwhelming feeling of elation after that flight, because I had achieved something that a few short months ago did not seem in the realm of possibility.

When my son came home for spring break, I decided to present his graduation gift to him. I went to the airport by myself while a friend drove him. He was so excited when they came upon the car dealership, for he was certain he was getting a new car. Turning into the airport, he became very excited; for he was positive Mom had bought him a plane. When he walked in, I explained that he was to give me a flying lesson. He had his CFI and CFII, so legally I was able to fly with him. Because he knew of my fear of flying, he was sure his mom had finally lost it. Eventually, I showed him my logbook to prove I had soloed. After the initial shock wore off, we did a preflight. The ultimate thrill of my life was taking off with my aviator son seated at my right—almost relaxed. We cruised around the practice area, and then he directed me to return to the airport for a landing.

The pressure was on; my landings were sometimes less than perfect. The concept of setting up the proper glide profile, looking far down the runway, and flaring at the proper moment had been difficult for me to master. I prayed that even if I never made a "greaser" again, I would do it then.

On final, ten feet above the ground, everything looked good— at least to me. By this time, my son, the CFII was twitching his hands and feet. "Tom," I said, "keep your hands in your lap and your feet off the rudders. I will land this plane." And land it I did—a real greaser. He was so stunned that he told me to do it again—and again—which I did!

After taxiing to the ramp, he was able to write in his logbook, "Flight with my mom." His entry in mine read, "Flight with Tom." You see, I was his first student!

Tom encouraged me to continue with my lessons, and on June 7, 1990, this white-knuckled flyer received her private pilot's license.

Earliest Recollections
Win Sluyter

"Dad, Mom, everybody: Look at the airplanes!" But no one except me wanted to see the airplanes. Dad would not stop; he just looked straight ahead and kept on driving. You see, occasionally there would be barnstormers in fields, looking for people to take rides, but we always drove right on by.

I was in love with flying and wanted to find out all that I could. I looked up "flying" in the encyclopedia and found out how airplanes worked. I read about early aviation and read every book that promised to have airplanes in it. I read about Lindbergh, and WWI flyers and their airplanes.

"What are you going to be when you grow up?" the older folks asked.

"An aviator," was always my answer.

I put a plank across my wagon for a wing. I used a pick to serve as a rudder bar and the handle was my control stick. A stack of Model-T tires became the cockpit. A road map was my chart, and I was off on imaginary flights to everywhere the map showed a flying field. I rehearsed the controls until I actually believed I was ready to fly.

Later on, at 14, I went to Put-In-Bay, a small resort island in Lake Erie's western basin, on a high school class trip. I told Mom the first thing I was going to do was go out to the airport for an airplane ride. She forbade me to do this and said that if I was going to fly, I could not go with the class. I did not mention it again. I had made up my mind. The first thing my buddy and I did when the Put-In-Bay steamer docked at Put-In-Bay was rent a tandem bike and head for the flying field. They had some Ford Trimotors and a big old Standard biplane painted black.

"We want to go for an airplane ride!"

"Rough or smooth?"

"Rough!"

"Give me a buck apiece and climb in."

We got into the front cockpit, and he got into the back one. The front could hold at least four people, but it was just my buddy, Roy, and I and our Brownie box cameras. We were going to be aerial photographers. With no seat belts, we stood up to see better over the sides.

He flipped us all over the sky while we shot pictures—double exposures and blurred images—as we tried to focus and forgot to advance the film. The pilot was having fun with us. He had us weightless, and then we slammed back down into the seat. I still have the pictures and the camera, too. The pictures were not too good, and I regret that we failed to take a single picture of the plane.

Mom found out, but she eventually got over it when she finally realized that she could not stop me. I was going to fly!

Forever Young
Verne Reynolds

1923! What a great year to be born! A sightseeing hop in a Jenny would set you back two dollars; the Charleston was the name of a dance, not just a city anymore; Lucky Lindy had not yet begun to think of Paris. Los Angeles didn't know anything about smog, Henry Ford thought black was a great color for all of his cars, and the market was destined to go higher ... for a while. It was a time when the future teased and enticed us.

Even now, on a quiet night, if you listen carefully you may still hear a soft echo of the twenties, a wisp of flirting laughter and the melody of some nearly forgotten piano. An echo that shimmers with black-beaded dresses cut high above the knee, close-cropped boyish bobs swept up tight against the cheek, spots of rouge and garters, and a hint of bathtub gin. But the echoes and the memories are foggy, like a mirror caught in steam.

When the children of the twenties were young, a surge of them flocked to our airfields determined to learn how to outfly their German heritage and cleanse the Pacific of its threat. I was one of them, and in a glimmer of memory, I still see myself standing there, a gawking silhouette, watching the magnificent patient Stearmans cough and float and dance at landing time in a slow, wing-bending pirouette. In the smudge of memory, I still feel the jolt of an inverted seat belt while my toes stretch for rudder pedals. And I recall the magic of helmet and goggles and parachutes, and how we ached to tell our girlfriends how wonderfully we flew.

Then the war ended. We picked up the pieces of our lives and went on to search for patterns of success, for fulfillment. I chased my own identity through a quarter century of trial and error, shackled to the earth, estranged from the ecstasy of flight. Then one day, above the pastures and the concrete ribbons, I flew again, with comfort this time. With cabin heat and yokes and flaps and buttons, I flew! The joy of earth and sky and the silver lace of clouds were there again, but somewhere in the corner of my memory, I kept remembering an open cockpit, where the wind whipped crisp and chilled against my cheek. It beckoned me and tugged at me. Then it happened.

A Starduster! Starduster Too! A two-place, open-cockpit biplane! In the hangar, waiting to be bought, with only a few hours on the airframe and engine, it seduced my imagination. I yearned for that open cockpit! I could ill afford the asking price, but I wanted it. I was falling in love, yet I hoped I could change some things. I wanted the cockpit lines recut, a cleaner shape for cowl and leggings, a new paint scheme, a new "N" number to satisfy my special whim. So, through metalwork, paint, and registration, Starduster Too, N1923S, *23 Skidoo* ... was born, tangled with the echoes and the soft memories of Rudy Valley, Jack Armstrong, Kay Kayser, the N3N, and Glenn Miller ...

As the ink dried on my payment check, and Skidoo rolled from its hangar for that first checkout flight, I knew afresh the coupling of a buyer's remorse and an owner's joy. Anxiety time. But, time to fly!

In anticipation of this moment, I had had several recent flights in a Citabria. It was the only way I could build taildragger time again. I was to learn quickly, in retrospect, that Citabrias and Stardusters have too little in common to be of much help. Now, with me strapped down tightly in the rear cockpit, and my well-meaning mentor occupying the front ... the time had finally come.

Too inexperienced to estimate what problems might follow; too rusty with prop pitch and manifold-pressure readings; with too much pressure to solo from a narrow, downhill runway in quiet air with 100-degree temperatures; too low in the cockpit to see effectively; too insecure to insist on better conditions; with too much anxiety, hope, and fear, I started the engine and began my check-out flight.

My mentor/instructor/checkout pilot had a Starduster of his own. He was *experienced*. He knew Skidoo and had flown most of its lifetime hours, but he was casually unprepared for what happened on our second landing, when both tail springs flew off during the bounce and rollout. Sitting in back, I wasn't sure of anything except that I had lost control. I had no rudder control, no control of the tail wheel. My mentor waited for me to make corrections. I waited for him to take over. We both thought the other person would work us out of the instant mess we were in. He could not hear my plea for help above the engine noise, and we were curving harshly toward a ditch on the left side of the runway. I stomped right rudder again... nothing worked! I was sitting too far back in the cockpit to reach full rudder and brake. I was in mid-panic when my checkout pilot finally slammed on the brakes, just as we left the runway and hit the graveled edge. We skidded sideways to a stop.

Now we were almost entirely off the runway, but with enough of our aircraft still encroaching to be a hazard to other landing traffic. My mentor aggressively tried, with full power, to twist and maneuver the Duster back onto the runway, but his abrasive efforts blew a tire, split the wheel fairing, splintered the legging, and broke the tail wheel brace. He shut down the engine. We clambered from the cockpits to inspect the damage. I anguished. My dream was shattered. Skidoo was broken. I wasn't sure what had gone wrong, or what I could have done to keep it from happening. I ached with helpless impotence. I had failed, and I was afraid.

We walked back up the runway, and there, on either side of the centerline, were the two tail springs that had not been securely fastened. The cause of the failure was now clear, but it left me burdened with remorse.

More time. More money. More remorse. But then, finally, I tightened the last bolt. My mentor flew N1923S to Santa Monica to meet me, and I put Skidoo in the hangar for a time of celebration. The bird was home, in the nest, at last.

I rebuilt the seat so I could better reach the rudder pedals and brakes. I taxied Skidoo around the airport until I felt that I understood the ground handling characteristics better. I could not delay the checkout flight much longer, so I hired an ancient, confident, and crinkled instructor who had thousands of hours in biplanes. We flew the pattern for about an hour, then he tied his seat belt and shoulder straps together, threw me a crinkled smile, and in spite of my earnest protests—he *walked away*! I was on my own.

I taxied Skidoo to the end of the strip, wiped my sweaty palms against my nervous thighs, and waited for tower clearance. Maybe I should taxi back to the hangar. Maybe I could say the wind had changed or the aileron felt loose or I had developed an instant cramp in my big toe or that I had a strange ringing in my ear.

"Two, three, Sierra, cleared for takeoff. ... "

Dumb. I waited too long. Now I had to go. I lined up with the centerline, asked for some Divine Guidance (with no assurance I would get any), held the stick all the way forward and pushed the throttle for full power.

Steady with the nose now ... a little more right rudder ... hold it steady ... straight ahead ... that's it ... the tail is up! Oops! Not too much ... there ... back again ... and better ... now ... easy ... back on the stick ... and then the smudge was gone! The ground fell away, and sky rushed between the runway and 23 Skidoo.

Alone, just the two of us slashing our way upward with each propeller bite through the haze of Los Angeles, gaining altitude. Drop the nose now ... hold it ... 85 ... that's good ... crosswind turn already? Bank it ... hold it steady ... keep the climb ... and downwind at pattern altitude. Ease back on the throttle now ... back some more ... that's right ... 18 inches of manifold pressure, 100 miles an hour, downwind opposite the tower.

"Two, three, Sierra, number three to land. ... "

Number three? Oh Gawd! What if I miss the airport? What if I can't find the other traffic? I didn't see any other traffic! What if I come in too high, too low, too fast, and too slow? What if I land crooked? What if I ground loop? What if I bend a wing or break a wheel? Maybe ... maybe if I just keep on flying straight ahead, downwind, and never return—I will never have to land, never have to know.

But, there's my traffic, well set up on final, time for me to turn for base leg. Ease off the throttle ... bank ... keep the nose down ... not too slow. That's it ... stabilize at 90 ... just a bit. The base looks good ... now bank again, and there's the runway, straight ahead. Whoa! Picking up too much speed! So raise the nose ... now the runway disappears! I know it's down there, somewhere straight ahead, but flying from the back, that long cowl hides everything. Tip it over just a bit … gentle slip. Ah, there it is … looks good! Just add a teensy bit more power now, make sure we've got the numbers made. Looks good now, kill the throttle, round out the slip. … Oops! Picked up too much speed! There! That's the right height. Now flare! No—too much stick! We're ballooning! Drop the nose again. Not too much. Now flare … hold it back. You're still flaring high, Dummy, but it's settling. Hang on. Here it comes! Right now! Where's the ground? Where is—thrrrrrrrump—that's it! We're down!

Now hold it steady, no ground loop. Keep the stick back. Are we going straight? I can't tell, and I can't see! I can't tell if we're going parallel to that line over there, or if we're angling toward it … or away from it! Slow it up … a little more brake … good. Slower now … slow enough; angle off between the lights—not over them. Ten miles an hour, five … and a little more brake … we've stopped.

We did it! We just erased 27 years of smudge! The shiver in my kneecaps and my pounding pulse testify that the smudge is gone. We did it! We flew! We really did it! We made it work, *Skidoo*!!

That tension-filled flight was the transition from prelude to pleasure. For years after that, N1923S filled my absorbing soul with a tangle of anxiety and joy, of poetry and song. We learned how to touch as lovers touch, at first with hesitation and then with exuberance. We chased the blur of our propeller through haze and sunlight, raced the wind past mountaintops, played leapfrog with the clouds, and looped and snapped and screamed down to chase innocent cattle and old friends. We tipped and swung and held the world inverted on silver threads of music. Each time we were together, each time the wind was crisp and brushed my cheek, it swept away the smudge, and I was young again. I was young again!!

I was Forever Young …

Missing an Airliner
John W. Carlson

"Sorry, guys, we're full."

I thought those four words grounded my dream of flight once again. It was 1964, the day of my 14th birthday, and for at least half those years, I had breathed, slept, dreamt, eaten, drunk, and lived for airplanes. What I had not done was actually *fly* in one. But this day, a Saturday that dawned a brilliant autumn blue, my father had driven me to Cleveland Hopkins Airport to rectify that situation. There, the kindly folks of American Airlines were cramming one of their new Boeing 727s full of excited riders who, for a nominal sum, would briefly loft these adventurous souls on an introductory flight into the skies of northern Ohio.

And now, I had missed it.

The ride back home in our boat-sized Chevy was a depressing one, as my father assured me that my first flight would be any day now. As for me, I was moodily pondering my cousins—kids for whom an elevator was something you rode in at Higbee's Department Store—who had already taken wing long before me.

Then Dad smacked the steering wheel and spoke three words I have never forgotten.

"The Nimrod Club!"

"Huh?" I asked, but by then he was already tearing into the countryside past woods and farmhouses and fields of ripening corn from which a lonely, grass airstrip—one with a single Cessna 180 parked on it—eventually emerged.

The Nimrod Club, it turned out, was a skydiving club. Climbing from the car, we scanned the air for signs of life and found the objects of our search. Jumpers! Three human specks were descending from on high, drifting and swaying beneath their silken, mushrooming canopies. Soon we noticed the sound of a motor growing ever louder, and then another Cessna 180 slipped over the cornrows at the far end of the strip and rumbled across the ground to where we had parked.

To my young eyes, the craggy pilot who climbed from this marvelous machine seemed the embodiment of aviation skill and lore and experience, though I realize now he was probably all of 35 years old. My father walked over, they exchanged a few words and then a few dollars.

"He's going up to spot the jumpers," Dad explained, smiling. "We're going along."

With that, the three of us headed for the second 180, an airplane differing from the 180 that had just landed in one vital respect— seats. Swinging into its cockpit, we belted ourselves in as the starter ground and the propeller began to windmill.

Nearly forty years later, I confess the details of that first takeoff have melded with memories of so many others. There is the wonderful, unique aroma of the cockpit, the engine's roar as the pilot pushed the throttle to the stop, the bounding rush as we sped across the grass, and then—unbelievably—the velvety climb as our metal wings caught lift.

Flying!

The rest of the flight remains fixed in my mind. His eyes peeled for the sight of their parachutes on the ground below, our pilot would spot a jumper and dive, and then zoom into the air above them so people in pickup trucks would know where to retrieve them. Whether this was standard operating procedure or a way to impress the youngster in the backseat, I do not know. Don't care, either. I still keenly remember the stomach-tickling thrill, the grins passed between my father and me, and the fact that much too quickly we were descending from the blue toward that little grass strip and then bouncing across its ruts.

As I recall, the drive back to our home in Elyria was as quiet as the one heading away from Cleveland's airport had been earlier. But this time it was quiet for a different reason; I was silently contemplating the special gift my father had given me for my 14th birthday.

Only two years later, I would be making my own way through the sky, cramming the knowledge of meteorology and air regulations and flight principles, which would later earn me my private pilot's license. But the lesson that day remains one I've never forgotten.

Sometimes, missing an airliner is a fortunate thing!

Picking Up Trains
John E. Jenista

It happened a long time ago (in 1934 actually), but the memory is still vivid in my mind. Way back then, my father was an early aviation enthusiast. He bought a war-surplus, Canadian-built Curtiss "Jenny." These were called "Canucks" in those days. Dad was a Cicero, Illinois, policeman and kept his airplane at the Laird Factory on Cicero Avenue. The field was called Ashburn Airport, and then later, the Chicago Flying Club. He would go to the airport early in the morning and get in a bit of flying before reporting for duty with his police force. His "weather check" at the field consisted of throwing a stone straight up into the air, as hard as he could. If he could see the stone all the way up on its path, the weather was good enough for flying. Things were much simpler in those days.

In 1933, the outside of the airplane needed to be recovered. He and my mother did the work, with Mother handling all the necessary sewing. When the job was done, Dad invited Mother to hop in and go along on the test flight. After all, what better way for her to check out her sewing job. She answered that "no way" was she going to fly with him and leave their children behind. If anything happened, there would be no one left to care for the kids.

"OK" said Daddy, "If you won't fly with me, my kids will."

He put my older brother (then five years old) and me (four years old) in the front cockpit of the Canuck, and off we went. I was absolutely thrilled to be in this real airplane with my dad and big brother.

Now there is something that you have to understand about little children. They do not have very much depth perception. Their brains have not yet developed the ability to accurately tell the difference between something big that is far away and something small that is up close. I can remember the noise and the wind as we became airborne. A short while later, I looked over the right side of the cockpit and saw the neatest little train out there. I wanted to play with it, and I reached my arm out of the plane to pick it up. Every time I reached out, the slipstream would whip my arm back. I began to cry in frustration, and Daddy thought I was afraid. He returned to the field and landed. It was only when he was undoing the seat belt that he realized that I was wailing, "I can't pick up the train, I can't pick up the train!" Everyone had a good laugh at my frustration, but my love of flying has remained strong from that day to this.

Fear of Flying
Leslie Green

To begin with, I do not like flying.

I am the kind of person who prefers a few Scotch & Sodas before boarding. Although I am not a religious person, I have been known to say many, many prayers in the waiting area while buckling up for takeoff, and I've been known to utter a variety of pleas for forgiveness during the landing as well. I do not like flying.

I tried to alleviate this irrational fear (you're supposed to be safer in a plane than in a car) by undergoing a brief treatment called systematic desensitization. Joseph Wolpe invented this program that helps you get over your fear of flying by imagining that you're in flight. I completed the course and thought I was handling this flying thing remarkably well. I boarded the plane where I would be confined for the three and a half hour trip to Oregon, settled back in my chair, ordered a cup of coffee, and said hello to the passenger next to me. "Did you hear about the big crash in Chicago?" he asked me.

I do not like flying, so it came as quite a shock to me that I agreed to fly Norman Seaton's two-seater airplane.

We drove out to Phil Hudson Airport, in Mesquite, where Norman had his airplane, "Yankee," parked.

I was impressed with Norman's thoroughness in the preflight check. The oil, gas, tires, wings, and flight controls all received his careful inspection. It was when he pushed the aircraft out of the hole in which it had entrenched itself in that I became doubtful.

"How did you move that?"

"Oh, it's easy. It doesn't weigh very much. See?" Norman demonstrated by lifting the tail end up.

I *do not* like flying.

"Do you want to shout to each other, or would you prefer a headset?" Norman asked.

Shouting? In a plane?

"Oh, I guess the headset will be okay," I said uncertainly. Then Norman instructed me as to the proper way of getting into a plane. I took off my high-heeled shoes, stood on the wing, and climbed into the seat. In front of me was a panel of instruments, a wheel, and two pedals. The panel of instruments looked like something only pilots of 747s are allowed to operate. It had approximately 18 indicators. The advertisement for this aircraft boasts "We put everything where you can see it and touch it easily with our Quick Scan panel." Quick scan is hardly the phrase I would use.

I buckled up while Norman began the arduous task of explaining the various instruments. "This is the speedometer, this is the temperature, this one tells you that you're turning, this one tells you how high you are, this one …. "

I hoped Norman did not expect me to remember all of them. I decided it was unwise to mention the troubles I'd had learning about the stick shift and clutch in my Volkswagen.

We taxied onto the runway, and naturally I attempted to use the steering wheel. "That wheel isn't going to do you a bit of good until you're in the air. You've got to use both pedals. When you want to go left, use the left pedal. When you want to go right, push the right pedal."

It seemed simple enough, but old habits are hard to break. Despite repeated warnings to "get my hands off the wheel" accompanied by mild threats of "making me sit on my hands," I persisted in hanging onto the only thing that looked as if it could control the aircraft. Norman, however, was patient, and he helped me steer the plane into takeoff position—using the pedals, of course.

"Now, we're going to bring the engines to full power and go straight down the runway. When the airspeed reaches 80 miles per hour, s-l-o-w-l-y pull back on the wheel," Norman instructed. Then he ran the engines up. I understood why we needed the headsets. It sounded as if we were in the middle of a hurricane. I slowly pulled back on the wheel, and the plane climbed upward. Airborne, at last!

The exhilaration and excitement of flying is unmatched. I can't really think of anything that is comparable. Yet along with the excitement, I must admit there were a few problems. Norman had told me not to raise the nose of the plane so high. I responded by pushing in on the wheel plunging us downward. Norman was remarkably cool under pressure. He leveled the plane off, and we soared eastward. I mentioned that I would like to fly over my parents' home. Norman looked down for visual reference. "Turn right, Leslie."

I know how to follow directions. Without hesitation, I turned the wheel sharply to the right. From down below, Norman's plane probably looked like it was competing in the annual air show.

"Uh, Leslie," Norman said as he leveled the plane off, "turn slowly the next time I tell you to turn." That seemed like a reasonable request. It was a little difficult steering sideways, anyhow.

The rest of the flight was uneventful and fun. All too soon it was time to land. Now, there are three basic steps in landing. The first one is to approach the airport. Next, you level the aircraft and then fly down to the runway. It sounded easy enough, but the plane was going downward, and below us was a pool of water.

"Norman, I know you're the instructor, but don't you think it would be a good idea to stay a little higher? Norman, I think we're going to hit that water. Norman, I don't want to land the plane. Norman, I think it's time to pull up. Norman!"

Norman ignored the hysterics of this student and landed the plane anyway.

"When's my next lesson, Norman?" I asked as I climbed out of the plane.

"I've got a pretty heavy schedule," he replied. "Christmas is coming up. And then there's spring break. And I'll be gone all summer and …."

And Set You Gently Back Again
Rick Geyerman

I had just returned from the pilots' weather briefing. We'd been given permission to launch and were unloading the chase truck when a red minivan slowly crunched to a stop in the gravel alongside us. The van carried the logo of a local television station. I'd been advised earlier that this TV station was sponsoring our balloon at this rally.

"Is this Carmen Miranda? The balloon?" He struggled to shoulder the TV camera.

Close enough. "Are you my passenger?" I stuck out my hand. "I'm Rick … Dave's my crew chief, you'll meet the rest later." I patted the carrybag. "This is Chic-I-Boom. Jimmy Buffet wrote a song just for her '… had bananas and mangos all piled to the sky. No, they don't dance like Carmen no more. …'"

"I won this ride in a drawing back at the station," he volunteered. "I'm pretty nervous. I was out drinking all night to screw up my courage … I'll be OK."

I couldn't tell if he was trying to reassure himself or me. We don't normally get to choose our passengers. We pilot five of the world's most famous special-shaped hot air balloons. Our balloons are the stars of the show. The sponsors, who provide money for the rally, and other VIP's usually, reserve our flights for themselves. Sometimes, it's the company president and sometimes, it's the company guy who pulls the lucky number out of the hat. I had a feeling that right now this guy wasn't feeling so lucky. The combination of the hangover and nervousness had drained most of the color from his face, except for that locked in the veins of his bloodshot eyes.

I busied my crew with preparations for launch. They spilled the balloon from its carrybag and spread it in the grass downwind from the wicker basket. I laid the basket on its side and began attaching the cables, carabineers, and fuel hoses that make the thing fly. I hitched the basket to the back of the truck with a safety rope because there was no sense in taking off before we were ready.

The crew knew what they were doing, but I went over each step on the checklist for the benefit of my passenger and his camera. He stayed plenty far back from the action but kept the tape rolling. I explained the crown line and how it would stabilize Chic-I-Boom as she first stood upright. I showed him the Velcro vents; sealed now, they'd be opened after landing to help empty the air from the balloon.

I gave leather gloves and arm protectors to the two-crew members holding the open mouth of the big balloon, and cranked the starter rope on the fan. "Balloon material is like a nylon jacket ... melts if it gets too close to the flame." I had to yell over the roar of the engine. "First, we fill the envelope with cold air. Then, we'll have room to shoot the flame without getting too close to the fabric."

Several times we walked the perimeter of the balloon, watching the giant bananas, grapes, and apples of her headdress fill with air and double-checking vents to be sure they were properly sealed. Even lying on her back, Chic-I-Boom inflates to about three stories. "We have to catch them before they get too high."

He nodded. The camera nodded.

Someone released a black helium balloon the size of a basketball, and the call "Pibal!" echoed across the launch field. Pilots stopped what they were doing and looked.

"Pibal," I said. "Pilot balloon. We watch where it goes and how fast and whether it changes direction as it rises. Whatever the wind does to that balloon, it's going to do to us once we get in the air." The look on his face made me sorry I'd reminded him. "Are you sure you want to do this?"

"Have to," he said. "I won the drawing. *And*, they gave me the camera."

We made a final circuit and got a "thumbs-up" from each crewmember. I settled behind the burners and spun the valves of the three 10-gallon propane tanks strapped securely into the corners of the basket. I opened the handles to the pilot lights and popped the buttons on the electronic ignition. Both flames hissed to life. I stood and made a final survey of the crew and the people watching. Everything was under control, and the crowd was well back from any danger. So far ... so good.

The balloon was packed tightly with air, and the mouth crew was ready. "It's gonna be loud," I warned, and throttled open the brass valves of the big dual burners. The flame they throw can heat an auditorium, and the sound they make—if you're not used to it—will cause small children to cry and dogs to tuck tail and run. My passenger jumped five feet and almost dropped his camera.

I burned for about four seconds and then levered off. "Mouth crew OK?"

I got two quick nods before they turned their faces again, and leaned away from the heat they knew was coming. I teased the burners on and off, filling heat when I could, then waited until the balloon reshaped herself, and I could add heat again. Steadily, hot air filled the envelope, and Chic-I-Boom began to rise. She's an impressive sight. My rider should have gotten some great film. The envelope strained at the cables, and as she stood, Chic-I-Boom pulled the basket upright beneath her.

"Weight on!" As the balloon rose high overhead, the crew came to help hold the basket aground. There were a dozen other balloons already in the air, drifting to the east, following the pibal on "gentle breezes" (the kind balloon pilots pray for). It was going to be a beautiful day.

I nodded to my passenger, took his camera, and tucked it into the only corner of the basket without a fuel tank. He lifted his leg high over the side, and half climbed, half fell, into the basket. "This is where I like my women passengers to wear short skirts and high heels," I joked. He didn't smile.

I switched on my instruments, adjusted the altimeter, and stowed my flight bag. Dave helped with a final check of the radios. I opened the burners and 20-foot flames seared the morning air above us. My passenger ducked. Most people do.

I pulled on the red line and opened the parachute vent at the top of the balloon. We jerked from the ground and settled again. He grabbed at me. "Heat makes us rise," I explained. "But if we need to come down, I can let hot air out from the top with this red line. When I let go, it reseals itself."

He looked doubtful. I promised. I showed him where to hang on—to the basket handles or the sides of the aluminum tanks—and cautioned him against touching the cables, ropes, or fuel lines.

Then I made Dave pull the ignition keys from his jeans. More than one pilot has stranded his crew by taking off with the keys to the chase vehicle in his pocket.

"Hands On!" The crew let up on their weight, but kept hands on the sides of the basket … there if we needed them.

I burned, testing for buoyancy. Quickly, we reached equilibrium. The lift of the hot air exactly equaled the weight of the two of us and the fuel in the basket. We hovered six inches off the ground. Dave took one final scan of the sky and gave me two thumbs-up. I thanked the crew, pulled the release pin on the safety rope, and burned hard. It was time to go flying.

I burned steadily at first, watching forward as my passenger stood behind me. Chic-I-Boom climbed over the watching crowd and a row of skinny poplar trees. "Gotch'er camera going?" I turned to ask.

He wasn't there. Wait … Yes, he was. My passenger was hunkered on his knees in the bottom of the basket, arms outstretched and fists clenched tightly over the edges of the fuel tanks in opposite corners. He was stretched … spread-eagle and face down … between the tanks. He shook uncontrollably, knuckles white.

"This is never gonna work. Get me down! Now! Please?"

"OK, as soon as I can."

"I think I'm gonna throw-up."

"No you're not. You'll be fine."

"Oh, God … Please! I never should have done this," he shivered harder.

I hoped he wasn't going to have a heart attack. Hell, I'd never had a passenger like this. I hoped "I" wasn't going to have a heart attack.

I searched ahead … a parking lot full of cars … some houses … a windmill in a pasture full of cattle and calves, and then a stretch of power lines. At the speed we were flying, it would be at least half an hour before I could safely put him back on the ground.

"What about your camera?"

"Piss on the damn camera! Get me down now! *Ok? Please!*"

"It'll be a minute. What do your folks do?" I don't remember his answer. Actually, I didn't care about his answer; I just needed him to think about something besides how afraid he was.

Wicker baskets creak. It's their nature. Each creak made him catch his breath and not breathe again until he was absolutely positive we weren't falling. I've had nervous passengers before, but this was beyond anything I'd even seen in the movies. He was in absolute, uncompromising, and total panic.

I keyed my radio and told Dave that we'd be landing on the road just past the power lines. There was barbed-wire fence on both sides of the road.

"Be there to stop us," I told Dave. It wasn't a suggestion.

The sweat drained from my passenger's face, dripped off the end of his nose, and puddled on the floorboards of the basket. Thank God for the floorboards. They kept him from seeing through the bottom of the basket. I asked him about his job and his friends at work. I asked him whether he had any brothers or sisters.

I told him about my brother and sister and how we'd been carsick once, because my dad told us we would be if we read while he drove. Later, my mom told us that was malarkey. "You were sick because he convinced you that you should be. It's all in your head," she explained. "Convince yourself not to be."

I told him I'd been reading in cars ever since. I don't know if he heard me. Maybe the lesson was a little obscure. It's all in your head.

I told him about the houses and windmill and power lines, and the pasture with the critters, and that we'd be down as soon as we could.

His response was always the same: "Put me down. Please put me down. I'll never do anything like this again. *Please.*"

I told him about my training, about the four other pilots and balloons in our fleet, and about the cool places we'd flown. I didn't tell him that I was a fairly new pilot with fewer than 30 hours in my logbook.

I told him about a pilot I'd heard of who was killed on his first flight. (Stay with me here.) The flight went well enough, but he got run over by a truck, crossing the road to his chase vehicle.

I told him I didn't think it was my time to go yet ... so it couldn't be his time, either.

I prattled and blathered and jabbered for 20 minutes. I said anything to distract him. Anything to stop him from thinking about how high we were and how afraid he was. I told him anything to keep him from puking in my balloon.

He kept his head down and held on, spread-eagle between the two tanks. He never loosened. A lesser metal would have crumpled like gum foil. He just kept begging me to put him down.

Eventually, we crossed over the power lines, and I hauled the redline hard to lose altitude. I could see the chase truck on the road ahead and my crew pulling on their leather gloves as they spilled from every door. The basket snagged briefly on the top strand of a fence, and as we jumped the ditch, I yanked the redline again. We slammed hard in the middle of the road, tipped slightly forward from momentum, and then straightened. The crew kept us from moving again.

"What's he doing down there?" asked Dave.

"Bumped his knee when we hit the fence." I knew it sounded stupid as soon as I said it, but Dave is "smart crew." Smart enough to ask questions when he should. And, smart enough not to when he shouldn't.

I nodded at my man on the floor. As sick as he was, he recovered quickly back on terra firma.

Fast recovery—a good trait for TV people. He hopped up and threw a big grin on his face. "Jeez, that was great!"

I nodded. His secret was safe with me. I figured that what we had up there was sort of like a doctor/patient relationship, strictly *confidential*. Besides, he had the camera, and it was his story. He could write it any way he wanted. There just wasn't going to be a lot of flight footage.

The road was wide and the winds soft, and Chic-I-Boom laid down in a tarp on the road. Dave and I took our time packing the basket gear, and by the time we were finished, the crew had snaked

Chic-I-Boom into her bag. I'd made sure the camera was filming again.

At the end of every flight, after the heavy work is done, we always perform the same ceremony. Gathered in a quiet group, one of us recites the Balloonist's Prayer:

The winds have welcomed you with softness.

The sun has blessed you with his warm hands.

You have flown so high and so well

that God has joined you in your laughter

and set you gently back again,

into the loving arms of Mother Earth.

Then, I tell the story of early ballooning in France in the late 1700s ... the local farmers, fearing invasion, often attacked and destroyed the landing craft and its "alien" passengers. Balloon pilots began to carry French wine (Champagne) to prove that they were actually human and friendly. We still carry Champagne today to prove that we are human and friendly.

For tradition, then, we open a bottle—Catch the cork! It brings luck!—And soft drinks for those who prefer. Then, we toast our new riders.

We did it all, just like that, for the camera.

The red van found us, and his wife emerged to join us for Champagne. The camera rolled. No doubt, she made the evening news.

He packed the camera, folded himself into the van, and lowered the window. "Hey, Rick. Thanks for the ride," he hollered.

"Anytime," I hollered back. "Anytime."

Terrified But Willing
Johnny Chakerian

While teaching stalls and spins to a student in an old T-Craft, I discovered that I had completely lost control. The student was okay with the stalls, but the spin scared him out of his wits. I kept yelling, "I got it!" But he wouldn't let go. (The T-Craft is a two-seat tandem airplane in which I sit in the back.) The ground was coming up fast, and the student had a death grip on the stick with it back close to his heart. The old T-Craft has a fire bottle mounted in the cockpit above us and between the seats. I hit him over the head with the fire bottle and he let go. Recovery was made with our wheels hitting sagebrush.

After this experience, I was hesitant when I received a call from a man who wanted to learn how to fly. He said he had joined the local flying club and was ready to get started. He also told me he was terrified of flying. So terrified, in fact, that the last time he had flown someplace he had to take a train home. I discouraged him, but he insisted on trying.

We met at the flying club the following weekend. He was a short, stocky, balding fellow in good shape. He had a lot of keys hanging on his belt and wore a San Francisco Giants baseball cap. I was impressed by how good of a student he turned out to be. In fact, during all of our meetings, he showed no sign of being afraid. I would have soloed him earlier if it were not for his previous comment.

One morning I stopped the airplane and started to get out. He said, "wait a minute!" and took the keys off his belt and gave them to me along with his wallet. He asked me to give them to his wife if he didn't make it back. I started to get back in the plane when he said, "No, I'm ready!"

He took off and left the area. He was gone longer then most students, but I wasn't worried until the phone rang in the hanger behind me and I was waved to come in. My heart stopped, I was now sure he had crashed. It was a call from another flying club member reporting a club airplane was buzzing the town! It was my student, the one "afraid to fly."

Who would have thought it? This was the same student who was so afraid to fly that he had to take a train home, and now I can't get him out of the cockpit. Much like another experience I had on a solo to another airport located just over some hills. One of my female students hit some rough air. It scared her so badly that she wet herself. For a much different reason, I couldn't get that student out of the cockpit either.

GOING SOLO

In soloing—as in other activities—it is far easier to start
something than it is to finish it.
— *Amelia Earhart*

I'm Ready?
Ralph Glasser

My first solo was memorable, as it should be for any new pilot, but the near calamity I experienced made it into a much better story.

I had accumulated about nine hours of dual time in the Cessna 152, operating out of Parks-Bi-State Airport (CPS, now called St. Louis Downtown Airport) in Cahokia, Illinois, just across the river and in the shadow of the St. Louis Gateway Arch. The day was clear and sunny, and for the first time, I failed to notice the stench of burning rubber from the tire recycling plant a mile away. My instructor, Bob Peyman, took me around the patch for some pattern work on runway 22, and as usual, I bounced my way through the touch and gos. After the third series of touchdowns, he had me make a full stop and taxi back to the terminal ramp—*where*, I might add, he scared the shirt off my back by opening the door and getting *out*.

"Take it around the pattern for a few touch and gos. You're ready! I'll be up in the tower," he said. Whereupon he promptly disappeared from under the wing leaving me helpless and unable to make audible, above the engine noise, the protests that were welling up in my throat.

The moment of truth had arrived. Although I did not expect it so soon, I knew I could never suffer having an instructor occupy the right seat indefinitely. With the meager reassurance of his professed confidence in me, I taxied back toward the end of runway 22 for my reckoning with the Sky Gods, mano-a-mano, wing-to-wing.

While taxiing the plane, I allowed a small bit of elation to enter my consciousness, momentarily steeling myself with exhilaration about the upcoming event. But, all too soon, it was dashed by confusion and the minor challenge now presented by the tower.

"Cessna 1234 Alpha, change runways; taxi to runway 4."

I had to stop, think about this, and then convince myself that it was "no big deal." Turning around on the taxiway, I acknowledged their instructions and got myself into position for my first solo departure.

The takeoff was quick. Too quick! I was startled with disbelief in my instruments and in the plane itself. That is until I realized that, weighing 200 pounds less, it was indeed conceivable that *I was actually flying*. And I was so very much alone. That first left turn seemed precarious. Surely the imbalance of having a vacant right seat would cause me to flip over and spin disgracefully to my demise. I remember leaning to the right while making the left turn to downwind hoping to help balance things. When Bob had been sitting next to me, did I lean unconsciously into him, away from the inside of those left turns? In a fully occupied C152, who could tell?

Once established straight and level on the left downwind for runway 4, I felt a bit better and even dared to look out the windshield to see the sights. And what a sight I saw! In a heartbeat, the sight of a light twin coming head-on, growing ever larger, and obliterating my view of anything else rapidly took up the windshield view. I instinctively wrenched the wheel to the right, guided by Divinity more than skill, and in my steep bank managed to miss the collision that was so imminent. If I had to guess, I would swear that it was a 90-degree bank, and the miss was no more than a wingspan. (Well, maybe with time the details have been embellished just a little.)

As quickly as I banked, I recovered, feeling more scared by the unusual attitude than by the collision I had narrowly escaped. I do not believe the other pilot ever saw me, as he was probably trying to assess the landing pattern from what he believed to be the proper right downwind for runway 22.

I continued on to make my first solo landing. Coincidentally, the tower mic was activated, and I overheard several people cheering in the background, presumably for me.

Buoyed by my recent success and my perceived accomplishment (A solo touch and go with only one bounce!), I continued around for the required set of three. After landing, Bob greeted me with more than the standard congratulations.

"That was incredible! Did you see how close you came to that twin? What a recovery!"

To this day, I am grateful that I wore my shirt casually that day. I am sure, had I tucked it in prim and proper, that when they cut off the tail, the lower posterior hem would have been stained. An embarrassing, indelible memento to document, for all posterity, that close encounter during my first solo in 1980.

One More Step
Jay Edmiston

Hot and oppressively humid, summer nighttime hangs like the ubiquitous kudzu draped in the trees of northern Mississippi. Dark green flight suits stick unevenly to the fledgling pilots strolling to their T-38s for yet another first in the interminable series of firsts that comprise Undergraduate Pilot Training. Flying our first nocturnal solos in the Talon, the Air Force's swept-wing, supersonic trainer, was just one more step toward the shiny silver wings we coveted.

By that point, we were three-quarters of the way through our yearlong training journey, and we had witnessed the departure of the last of our group; individuals who would never know the satisfaction of completing the program. The final washouts were usually dismissed for simply failing to master the Talon's tricky landing characteristics, becoming the ultimate victims of unrelenting demands on time and personal ability.

It was indeed a tough craft to land, at least at first. It was tougher still to earn any praise from ever-critical instructors positioned just a few feet behind you. A kind word was hard to come by, not so much for failure to achieve the required proficiency, but because landings had a way of stressing even the best instructors. They couldn't see forward, they couldn't see the student, and they damn sure wouldn't see their future if they let some novice land a few hundred feet short of the runway.

Watching the graceful form of a T-38 soaring across the sky, one would never expect the ride to be the rough and tumble jaunt it is. Smooth as silk in the straight and level, it shakes and rattles continuously during the final turn, swept wings working furiously at the high angle of attack required to successfully negotiate the curve.

Relentless instructional perseverance had taught us to see, avoid, and correct the dreaded high sink rates that could quickly develop if our attention wandered. Practice had given us the tools and developed our senses to the point where we could be trusted to fly this tricky machine—even in the dark.

Now settled into the final stages of the program, and assured of ourselves in the manner of young military pilots, we felt that the drill for the night was simple enough. Launching from the center most of three runways at Columbus Air Force Base, we rocketed off into the dark. Twin blue afterburners growing ever smaller in the distance; winking out first one then the other. It was a simple course. We were to fly straight out 30 or 40 miles, then turn leisurely following a semicircular path, and finally arrive back at the far side of the base some fifteen minutes later. Next, we would complete several touch and go landings before hanging it up for the evening. All in all, it was a short flight compared to most.

The moonless night gave us full value for our labors. The scattered ground lights looked much like stars amid the heavens. In fact, a dedicated inside and outside crosscheck was needed to keep one honest and to avoid confusing heaven and earth. If this had been a daytime flight, the undemanding cruise back to the field would have provided a perfect sightseeing opportunity. Below me in the dark lay hundreds of square miles of cotton fields dotted with the occasional dilapidated shack bereft of doors and windows. This is a vista that is permanently burned into my memory. I am continually humbled by the realization that those hovels still serve as homes to people too poor to imagine anything better.

Nearing the end of this circular tour, the fuzzy glow of the base suddenly comes into focus as it sheds its hazy covering. The colorful lights of the runway seem to settle upon the pointed nose as if to say, "Welcome home." Tranquil feelings vanish as quickly as student and Talon make their 300-knot trip down initial and pitch out in a hard, steeply banked right turn for the first landing.

Rolling out on the downwind leg, tasks must be completed swiftly and the aircraft slowed to configure for landing. Lowering the landing gear helps to further decelerate the jet as the comfort of the runway lights pass abeam the ship and steal from view; the lightless

Mississippi farmland taking its rightful place beneath the wings once again. Throttles are moved forward to catch the computed airspeed, flaps are lowered, and the nose begins its steep, descending turn back toward the airstrip.

Somewhere in the final turn of my first pattern, I lost track. I lost track of the colorfully outlined runway that was now too slowly returning to view over my right shoulder. I lost track of the ground, swallowed up in the black emptiness below. I lost track of how quickly my precision-machined express elevator was hurtling toward the ground floor. The moment of realization—when you know you are not in control—is like no other.

When that moment arrives, the brain shifts into overdrive, and the composite check of inside and outside references becomes the lifeline of the pilot. Only a second passed in the time it took me to regain my awareness and assert my superiority over the situation. It seemed like an eternity. Soon enough, I rolled out on final, aimed the jet square into the middle of the runway overrun, and flared into the stiff-legged thump of landing a few feet beyond the threshold. The nose is lowered, the power increased, and the plane leaps back into the sky for several more circuits of challenging, but uneventful, practice. Time short and fuel dwindling, it is time to return to earth. With a graceful touchdown, nose held high to slow it, the Talon completed its final landing.

Moving slowly to its parking spot, the sleek trainer slips in and out of the gathering wisps of ground fog. One more step taken toward graduation, young pilots head home, perhaps having learned lessons not found in the curriculum or shared with others, but buried deep within nascent aviator souls to be called upon during future occasions whenever darkness threatens to overwhelm.

Pearl Harbor Day Solo
Glenn Anderson

There are many reasons to remember Pearl Harbor Day, but for the remainder of my life I'll always remember it with great fondness. What an odd way to react to the remembrance of "a day that will live in infamy" as President Roosevelt called it. As it turns out, this was the day, 58 years after that infamous day that I soloed in an airplane just a couple months shy of my 60th birthday. I finally lived the dream that I had carried for most of my life.

In 1944, at the age of 4, I traveled with my mother by train (the Hiawatha) from Chicago to South Dakota to visit my grandparents. The train was loaded with Army Air Corps soldiers. One of these men removed his gold and silver collar wing insignia and gave it to me, a towheaded little boy. Something happened in that transaction that fueled a fire in me for aviation. On hot summer Sundays after the war was over, my father would take us to Midway Airport where we would watch the DC-3s take off and land. For me, it was a ballet of dancing airplanes.

When I was 17 years old, I joined the South Dakota Air National Guard. Looking back now, I see that this move was really an excuse to be around airplanes. Even though I was not flying, I was close to the action on the field. I took my first flying lesson that year, 1957, from a flying farmer in rural Larchwood, Iowa. The farmer's name was Mr. Zanger, and he owned a hand-propped Stinson. On the day of my lesson, we taxied the plane out of the barn and onto a nearby hayfield. I will never forget that feeling of total euphoria as the airplane leapt off the hayfield and Zanger said, "That was a great takeoff son."

I gulped and said, "I thought you were flying."

What a great day! Unfortunately, I was broke and in college, and as it turned out, my first lesson would also be my last for a long time to come.

In the late 1960s I tried it again but this time at the airport in Anderson, Indiana. I had about 12 hours dual time in a Cessna 150 when the money ran out—before my solo. Up until then, my only accomplishment, as I recall, had been getting my instructor airsick doing stalls.

Fast-forward to the late 1980s when I began lessons again. By this time, my oldest son had graduated from the U.S. Coast Guard Academy as well as Navy flight school and was a Coast Guard helicopter pilot. I added about another 10 hours of flight training, took ground school, and passed the written. But money ran out again. Still no solo.

Because of my interest in aviation, I became active in the Experimental Aircraft Association. Even though I didn't have the funds to fly, at least I would be around people who do fly.

In 1999 with a small financial windfall and encouragement from my wife Diane, as well as others, I took another serious run at making this dream a reality. Well, it all paid off on Pearl Harbor Day. My instructor checked my paperwork, signed me off to solo, and away I went. The first landing was flawless or at least it felt that way to me. The two that followed were OK. When we got back to the flying club, I was congratulated and had my ritual "tail feathers" trimmed. I don't think I could have been "higher" if I had been launched into outer space!

When I finally returned home after the flight, I went to the jewelry box where I had kept those WWII collar wings all these years and pinned them on my jacket collar. After over 60 years, I finally felt worthy of wearing them not only as a symbol of my personal rite of passage, but also in memory of all those men who flew, fought, and died during that conflict over 60 years ago.

Cross-Country Solo
Christina Naber

"Flaps down, check the hinges and nuts, lights aren't cracked, leading edge is—ugh, that's a lot of bugs! Fuel strainer shows no dirt or water, twenty-four gallons usable in each tank, oil is somewhat clean with six liters. Prop clear, spark plugs intact—Oh man, looks like they've been glued back on. Lovely. Right tire is good, shocks 3.5 inches, stall buzzer clear, tie down ropes removed, check left side, and empennage is free of hazards. Well, this is it."

This was my first solo cross-country and it was one hundred and fifty-two long miles. I'd be traveling alone at an altitude of five thousand feet. Preflight looked good, and now I was ready for the inside checklist. Without an instructor, I didn't want a flooded engine or a clogged spark plug, so I ran through it slowly as not to miss anything.

Everything was going great, the propeller was spinning, the engine was running well, and I began to feel those nervous, excited butterflies in my stomach. The kind most people get on a first date or when they've fallen in love. You see, I'm in love with airplanes. My friends think I'm crazy because I spend hours at the airport. One person who understands this love is my friend John, who flies even better than I do. When we go out, we don't just drive across town; we fly to Wisconsin or Indiana for a nice dinner and a view of the sunset at five thousand feet.

Back to my preflight. The engine was running fine with fuel flowing freely, so I reached over to turn off the fuel pump, the next item on my checklist. Out of habit I ran through my gauges and something caught my attention. The fuel pressure had fallen below the redline, indicating a possible problem. However, the engine was not coughing or sputtering. I turned the electronic fuel pump back on and saw the fuel pressure dive once more. At this point I was worried. I didn't want my graceful bird in the sky to turn into a falling rock, but at the same time, I didn't want to cancel my flight. It had been cancelled so many times because of weather, and I didn't want a fuel pump to hold me back. Then I thought about the consequences. What if my engine quit in the middle of nowhere? There's no reason to make flying dangerous, so I went slowly through the checklist to shut off the airplane and then climbed out to find a mechanic. (And people say teenagers have no common sense … whatever!)

I found one of the mechanics and drug him out to the airplane. As I explained my problem, I ran through the preflight check again. He stared at the gauges for a minute and said, "Hmm. That shouldn't happen." Not too reassuring when it's your airplane! He checked the engine and concluded that it was simply a gauge malfunction. So crisis resolved, I was signed off again to leave on my cross-country.

I reorganized my flight plan, started the engine, and prepared to taxi with every intention to closely monitor the fuel pressure. I taxied out to runway 11 and completed my run-up. I radioed for takeoff followed by a west departure at seventeen hundred. Soon afterward I called Kankakee Flight Service and activated my VFR plan. Then it was time to transition to DuPage's airspace. Meanwhile, I was following specific headings and altitudes, looking for traffic, and keeping a close eye on my fuel gauges.

As I watched the ground go by at one hundred knots, I remember how my little brother and I used to count the port-a-potties in the fields when my grandpa would take us flying. Well, here I was, all alone with the square fields five thousand feet below me and miles of sky above me. It was time to count the port-a-potties by myself. And I loved it! Until you've experienced it, it's hard to understand why pilots love to fly.

I made it to Whiteside/Sterling Rock Falls without any problems. That was the easy leg of my trip. My landing was pretty good, and I taxied my airplane into an empty parking space near the FBO. As I shut off the engine, I saw the line boy walking over to refuel my airplane and tie it down. He looked about my age—seventeen or eighteen. I took off my headset, opened the door, and stepped out of the plane. I was the last thing that kid ever expected to see climb out of a Warrior. A girl, for starters, alone in an airplane, who looks like she's twelve! He practically stopped in his tracks when he saw me. I couldn't help laughing. He asked if I needed fuel and how long I was staying. Then he added, "So, how old are you anyway?" I smiled and told him I was only fifteen and breaking FARs, so he shouldn't tell anyone I was there. He just stared in disbelief until I told him I was actually seventeen and on my first solo cross-country. We got to talking, and he told me I was the youngest girl he'd seen fly into the airport alone which was why he was pretty surprised; especially when I told him I came all the way from Chicago. Nice guy though—he let me use his phone to call flight service so that I could close my flight plan and file from Whiteside to Rockford to Schaumburg.

Minutes later, I said goodbye and was back in my trusty airplane, 8-1-Lima as we affectionately called it. The fuel pump was still running a little low. Since there wasn't much I could do about it, I took off from Whiteside and was on my way to Rockford. You can tell that you're entering Rockford's airspace because of the nuclear power plant towers and all of the jet traffic. The radio work was challenging. I had to talk to west tower, approach, tower, ground, clearance, tower, and east departure! Even with all of the work, it was a lot of fun. Especially since I got to land right behind a Citation V.

From Rockford back home to Schaumburg would be my hardest leg. Rockford east departure gave me a heading to follow which would keep me out of traffic. This messed up my course slightly because the new headings were different than what I had planned. To make matters worse, there were cities everywhere that made it difficult for me to find the checkpoints, and I had to fly low to keep out of O'Hare's airspace. (Go in there and lose your license—death to the aspiring pilot!) I ended up about five miles north of Schaumburg airport and had to follow Roselle Road back.

By the time I arrived at Schaumburg, the winds were out of the southwest at about 13 knots gusting to 20—a bit too much for a solo student. I wasn't even signed off for that amount of wind. However,

I had no choice but to land the airplane. I steadily entered the pattern on a left forty-five for runway 11 and followed all procedures. As I slowed the plane down to 75 knots on final, I felt a gust of wind. Instinctively I left in the third notch of flaps for airspeed. When I was about five feet off the runway, another gust of wind suddenly swept along the runway and my left wing dipped dangerously. I followed through on the controls and hit the rudder hard to maintain the centerline. The landing was a bit bumpy but pretty good for conditions. Whew, was I relieved!

Then I remembered I had to park the airplane, which happened to be the most challenging part of the flight. Since airplanes don't go in reverse it is not easy to back them into a parking place. I have to park in front of the spot and push the plane backwards relying only on my brute strength. It requires a little effort for my 98 pounds to move 2,000 lbs of metal and glass, but I can do it!

Back inside Schaumburg airport my chief instructor, Rick, was waiting for me. He congratulated me on my first solo cross-country and asked how it went. I told him everything was fine except the fuel pump. He smiled and said, "How about somewhere a little farther next time? Like Iowa?"

I smiled in agreement and his last words were, "Meet me in the left seat in five years!"

Hopping the Fence
Anson Jones

The year was 1967, the plane was a J-3 Cub, and my total flying time was 3.5 hours. As you can tell by all that experience, my first solo was interesting to say the least. The instructor, Mr. Hathaway, and I did a couple of touch and gos and then he got out. He said the usual, "Give me three more." And I was off. You know that feeling every new pilot gets their first time alone—just you and the plane and hopefully a *hand* on your shoulder. The takeoff was good, but that first landing was really something to write about. Naturally I came in fast and bounced it off the runway. A crosswind caused the Cub to turn into the wind, which was about 45 degrees off the centerline. I didn't even know what the rudder pedals were for except brakes. Before I knew it, I was headed out over a field with two-foot-tall grass and a fence line with shrubs and weeds six feet high.

My first fear was that if I banked to get back to the runway my wing tip would hit the grass and that would be it. My second fear was that if I pulled back on the stick I would stall, another option I didn't want to take. I just held it level, about three feet off the ground and headed straight for the fence. It was decision time, I pushed the stick forward, flew it into the ground, bounced, pulled back on the stick, and up over the fence I went. I finally got back and landed somewhere on the runway. I was proud and bullet proof. I was finally a pilot!

The look on the faces of my father and Mr. Hathaway is still very vivid in my mind—I thought they were both going to have heart attacks!

Falling for You
Ken Yellen

I learned to fly at Opa-Locka, a very large ex-military airport near Miami, Florida. When it was time to solo, I went around the pattern with my instructor a couple of times. Then he got out in the middle of the field and told me to "take it up." Since it was a nice, warm winter day in Miami, he lay down on the grass at the side of the runway and waited for me. Well, while he was on the grass, another pilot reported that someone had fallen out of an airplane and was lying on the field! Needless to say, airport security was called!

Cross-Country on Empty
Ken Heidger

Since I've worked on so many different aircraft, I thought it would be a good idea to learn how to fly. I soloed in Luscombe N1561K on June 30, 1951. Shortly thereafter, I planned for my cross-country, a 3-leg solo flight from Lawton to Altus to Frederick and then back to Lawton, Oklahoma. The rules stated that I stop only at each location just long enough to get signed-off; proof that I was there but nothing else, not even to refuel. I was slightly worried because my planned itinerary, including fuel consumption and changing wind directions, was not set up for flying in a triangle. I pressed on, confident that I had planned sufficiently enough to make the trip.

Everything seemed fine up until the last leg of my trip. As I left the Frederick airport, I noticed the fuel gage getting awfully low. About halfway to Lawton, the engine ran out of fuel. I had my eye on a small, fenced-in field that looked nice and green and was across the street from a large farm. I made a slow, nose-high landing, using up most of that pasture while trying not to hit the fence. After I was assured that I had indeed landed without harming the airplane or myself, I climbed over the fence in search of the resident farmer. After much explaining and a firm promise not to hit the fence on my way out, I returned to my Luscombe with five gallons of tractor gas.

Remembering the rules, I thought twice about refueling but came to the conclusion that this was an exception due to the fact that I was not at one of the assigned stops. I refueled and prepared for takeoff. I pulled the Luscombe up against a fence on one end of the pasture and got in with my fingers crossed. While at full brakes, I put in maximum power and then slowly released the brakes to start a takeoff roll—hitting every cow-made pothole in the field. The mind-rattling bumps became less and less as I slowly gained altitude and cleared the fence by only a few inches.

After landing at the Lawton airport, I parked the plane, took care of extra business, and headed out to my car. I caught a glimpse of my instructor in my car's rearview mirror. He was looking in the gas tank and scratching his head. Maybe he thought I was such a skilled mechanic that I must know something extra special about conserving fuel. Not a word was ever mentioned about the mystery fuel. I will always remember that flight as one of my most exciting adventures. I just hope I won't have another like it!

Captain Tow Bar & The Birds
Johnny Chakerian

On my first solo I looped the airplane. My instructor was also in the air and saw the whole thing. He came alongside and waved me in to land. I made a nice landing, but he was so upset he bounced clear down the runway.

Since then, I've had many students scare and impress me. I've loved every minute but sometimes I question some of their reasoning ability. Like the time I checked out an Air Force Captain in the club's T-34 Beechcraft. I was told the next morning that he had hooked up the tow bar to the front wheel of the T-34 and used it to pull the airplane out of the hanger. Then the Captain got in, started up, and taxied toward the runway. As he went by the tower, they called to inform him that the tow bar was still hooked up! Then he turned around and taxied back—with the tow bar still attached, bouncing up and down. Guess he thought his crew chief had removed it. At least that's what he said.

One of my favorite solo stories took place at Reedley College where I taught students to fly the school-owned J-3 Piper Cub. After summer break, a student came to the airport, did a preflight, and then took the airplane out for a spin. After landing, he taxied to the fuel pump and shut down. While gassing up, this student heard chirping coming from the engine cowling. He looked in to see a bird's nest between the magnetos. With eggs just hatched, the two little birds had just had their very first flight.

MORE TO LEARN

Now, there are two ways of learning to ride a fractious horse: one is to get on him and learn by actual practice how each motion and trick may be best met; the other is to sit on a fence and watch the beast a while and then retire to the house and at leisure figure out the best way of overcoming his jumps and kicks. The latter system is the safer, but the former, on the whole, turns out the larger proportion of good riders. It is very much the same thing in learning to ride a flying machine.

-Wilbur Wright, from an address to the Western Society of
Engineers in Chicago.
September 18, 1901

Climbing Through FL600
Lars Hoffman

I fell in love with the U-2 in the summer of 1992. While deployed to a classified location I watched with amazement one morning as a U-2 lifted off and pulled up to what seemed like a near-vertical climb. I was struck by the power and beauty of the mysterious black jet, climbing out of sight within minutes. I knew at that moment that I had to be a U-2 pilot.

The U-2 handles like no other plane in the US Air Force (USAF) inventory. It requires finesse and patience at high altitude and aggressive, exaggerated control inputs during flare and touchdown. U-2 pilots fly highly classified reconnaissance missions solo, at altitudes above 60,000 feet, while wearing a full-pressure suit, and often near unfriendly territory. Because of its unique handling qualities and demanding operational mission, the U-2 training squadron at Beale Air Force Base, California, thoroughly reviews the applications of prospective pilots and invites the highest qualified candidates for two weeks of formal interviews and a three-flight evaluation in the two-seat trainer U-2.

I finally got my shot in August 1993. First on the schedule were interviews with everyone from squadron pilots to the wing commander, a one-star general. The U-2 pilot community is a tight-knit group, known as the "Brotherhood." U-2 pilots share a unique professional bond and rely closely on each other during the long deployments. A second U-2 pilot serves as backup for every mission. They plan with the primary pilot and are prepared to step in should the primary pilot become unable to fly the day's mission. The U-2 pilot community wants to make sure that any new pilots admitted to their ranks will be someone they can rely on and work with under the most challenging conditions.

My first interview week also included a visit to the life support shop to try on the full pressure suit, similar to the one worn by Space Shuttle Astronauts. The exercise entailed donning the whole suit, closing the clear, bubble-shaped helmet faceplate and hanging out in the suit for about an hour. Having SCUBA dived before I remembered the strange feeling the first time I took breaths under water. I had the same feeling the moment they lowered and locked the faceplate. After a few moments I was able to relax and breathe normally.

The technicians left me alone sitting in a recliner. I heard a motor humming under the chair and assumed it was my oxygen generator. I was breathing 100% oxygen within the face cavity of the helmet. I became so relaxed in the recliner that I fell asleep … that is, until the motor under my seat suddenly stopped. I snapped awake and wondered if this meant I would stop receiving oxygen. I felt a twinge of anxiety as I tried to remember how to unlock and open the faceplate. But before breaking the airtight seal, I noticed that I was still able to breathe. I saw a technician approaching from the other room and quickly settled back into the recliner as if nothing had happened. Apparently I passed the "claustrophobia test" and was forwarded to the three-flight evaluation the following week.

My interview flights were a special experience. I was assigned to one of the top instructor pilots in the squadron to prep for my flights. I asked lots of questions and listened carefully to everything he said. When I got back to my room, I "chair flew" all of the procedures and techniques until I knew them cold. During my first flight the next day, I knew the procedures, but soon discovered why the U-2 is known as the toughest aircraft to land in the USAF inventory.

One of the many features that distinguish the U-2 from every other USAF aircraft is its bicycle landing gear arrangement. The U-2 landing gear consists of a main gear just forward of the wings and a tail gear. The wheels on the tail gear are no more than over-sized skateboard wheels, about 9 inches in diameter. During taxi operations, supporting spring arms with small wheels, known as "pogos," are fitted under each of the 50-foot-long wings. During takeoff they are designed to drop to the runway as the wings begin to lift.

Another unique feature of the U-2 is its 109-foot wingspan with high-lift airfoils. The wings were designed to do one thing, to lift the U-2 and its sophisticated sensors as high as possible during reconnaissance missions. This is great when you are trying to climb higher all day but it poses new challenges when trying to descend from 60,000+ feet to land.

The nickname for the U-2 is the Dragon Lady. The official story is that name came from a comic strip spy character. I think the name also applies to the way the U-2 handles in flight, the "Lady" at altitude turns into a "Dragon" at touchdown.

When people ask what it is like to land the U-2 I tell them to imagine sitting on a ten-speed bicycle in the back of a pickup truck as it drives down the highway at 70 mph. Suddenly, the tailgate opens and you roll out of the bed of the truck, touching down rear wheel first, then front wheel, while trying to gain control of a suddenly unstable bicycle that feels as if it wants to dive into the weeds at any moment.

To safely land the U-2, the pilot must bring the unwieldy craft over the runway threshold between 5-10 feet and then take it gently down to 2 feet above the runway surface and precisely hold it there as the airspeed bleeds off. The high-lift wings must be stalled as the tail wheels touch down first, then the main wheels. Even then the landing is not complete. The pilot must keep the wings from touching the runway while smartly slowing the Dragon Lady to a stop. Only then can the pilot allow a wingtip to touch the runway surface, protected by titanium skid plates under each wingtip.

In the U-2 community takeoff and landing are referred to as launch and recovery, owing to the support team that is required to get the pilot and craft safely airborne and back down. Two chase vehicles accompany every launch and recovery. A support crew follows the U-2 to the runway and accomplishes final checks before launch, including pulling the safety pins and pogo retaining pins. A second U-2 pilot monitors the whole operation and maintains radio contact from a high performance sports car. The sports car is critical during the landing phase when the chase pilot speeds in from the edge of the runway to call out critical information to the U-2 pilot attempting to land the "Dragon."

I survived the two-week interview process and garnered a coveted training slot. I returned in January 1994 to begin the 9-month checkout program for both the T-38 companion trainer and the U-2. Because there are so few U-2s in the inventory, pilots also fly the T-38 supersonic trainer to maintain their instrument proficiency. Every flight of the checkout program was memorable, but none compared to my first flight above 60,000 feet.

U-2 pilots wear a full pressure suit when they fly above 50,000 feet. At those altitudes the cockpit pressure altitude is around 29,000 feet, as high as Mount Everest. The pilot experiences that low pressure on his body throughout the flight. The pressure suit provides some relief from this fatiguing environment, but it is primarily worn to save the pilot's life should the cockpit suddenly lose pressure at high altitude. The pressure is so low above 63,000 feet that the pilot's blood would instantly boil if not for the pressure suit.

My first high flight was scheduled for 2 ½ hours over central California. I could hardly sleep the night before. I tried to imagine what the view would be like from twice as high as airliners fly. I had seen pictures around the squadron, but I was told those pictures didn't do justice to the actual view. After eating the standard "high protein-low residue" high flight breakfast, I headed to the life support shop to put on my full pressure suit.

Pre-flight preparations went smoothly and soon my instructor and I were suited up and headed out to our U-2. Before long, we were on the runway and ready for launch. Throttle up, brakes released, and before long we were climbing out so fast I could hardly read the altimeter. We passed airliner altitudes within ten minutes and soon passed 50,000 feet. I got a kick as we called out "climbing through Flight Level 600" to air traffic control.

I was so busy during the climb-out that I barely had time to look outside. Finally, my instructor took the controls so I could look around and enjoy the magnificent view. Wow! While climbing over San Francisco Bay I could see hundreds of miles in all directions. I was able to make out Mount Shasta to the north, Lake Tahoe to the east, and Yosemite Valley to the south. I was breath-taken by the view but my instructor reminded me that we had a full training schedule before heading home.

On that first high flight I learned many important skills including how to eat our specially prepared tube foods and drinks that U-2 pilots consume on 10+ hour flights and how to relieve myself using the cleverly labeled "urine collection device," or UCD, that I was wearing under my pressure suit. After completing my in-flight training, we started the hour-long descent to landing back at Beale.

I had gotten pretty comfortable landing the U-2 in a lightweight flight suit, but this would be the first time landing while wearing the bulky, 50-pound full pressure suit ... a whole new and challenging experience! After wrestling with the Dragon, I finally got her on the ground safely. I was humbled but relieved and couldn't wait to do it again.

You never really "tame" the Dragon Lady. I've flown over fifty types of aircraft in my Air Force career and the U-2 is the most challenging. I learned something new about the U-2 on every flight. Since that first high flight in 1994, I've had the great privilege to fly many operational and combat U-2 reconnaissance missions around the world but I'll never forget the thrill of that first time ... climbing through FL600!

Crossing the Pond
Jack Roosa

Incredible. That was how I felt when I was tagged to fly an F-16 fighter aircraft from a base in Germany to the United States. In pilot speak; I was going to get my first crack at "crossing the pond"—a non-stop flight over the Atlantic Ocean. It was a thrilling notion.

As the son of an Air Force pilot, I grew up hearing stories of aviation. I would hang on every word as my dad described flying fighters during the 1950s and 1960s. I remember one vivid description of his flight from Langley Air Force Base, Virginia, to Germany in an F-100 fighter aircraft. As I sat there, listening to his words of adventure, I quietly hoped that one day I would get the chance to experience such a thrill.

Well, that day arrived on a cool, fall day in Germany. I was flying with the 480th Fighter Squadron, based out of Spangdahlem Air Base, Germany. Our squadron was selected to participate in a flying operation called COPE THUNDER. COPE THUNDER was an aviation exercise designed to train pilots in a large-force flying event simulating combat conditions. The event was held annually at a base in central Alaska. Our squadron was tasked to fly 18 aircraft from Germany to participate in the event. To accomplish this task, we would have to fly the aircraft over the Atlantic Ocean, land in New York for a two-day rest stop, and then continue the journey to Alaska.

On the day of the flight, I arrived at the squadron at 0530, three hours before our scheduled takeoff time. It was a typical fall morning in Germany—cold and overcast with a light drizzle. The 17 other pilots and I gathered in the squadron briefing room to attend a predeparture flight brief. The briefing covered the route of flight, expected weather, NOTAMS, air-to-air refueling details, and other flight events. I could sense eagerness in the room as each of us mentally prepared for the transatlantic flight. After the brief, we collected our flight materials and moved into the life support room to suit up for the flight.

Now crossing the ocean is not like a normal training mission, so the garb I put on for this flight was much different than anything I had worn before. The route of flight was planned to carry us over the frigid North Atlantic. So, we had to dress for the prospect of ejecting out of our aircraft and landing in the cold ocean water waiting below. This required us to don an anti-exposure suit, affectionately known as a "poopy-suit." The poopy-suit can best be described as a rubberized, one-piece overall. It fits snuggly around the neck and wrist and is designed to keep water away from the body in the event we ended up bobbing around in the ocean. Although we all knew the suit was for our protection, it was difficult to put on and certainly uncomfortable to wear for any extended time. After struggling into the poopy-suit, the g-suit, flight jacket, and harness came next. Thirty minutes later, I was finally ready to walk out to the aircraft.

By the time I had arrived at my aircraft, the drizzle had developed into a torrential downpour. Thank goodness the jets were parked in Cold War era concrete shelters. At least I would stay dry as I readied the aircraft for the flight. After a quick walk-around, I jumped up into the jet, strapped in, and waited for the appointed start time. While waiting, I tried to arrange all the items in my cockpit into some usable fashion. The cockpit of an F-16 is fairly cramped to begin with, but when I added an extra canteen of water, a box lunch, a couple of sodas, and a newspaper to all of my flight materials, I found out just how small the space became.

At engine start time, I signaled the crew chief and fired up the motor. It was an uneventful start to an eventful mission. In order to fly all 18 aircraft to Alaska, the squadron leadership decided to break the 18 aircraft into three flights of six F-16s, each flight separated by 30 minutes. I was appointed as the fifth aircraft in the last flight. After cranking the jet, I patiently waited for the check-in on the radios.

All six aircraft were ready to roll at check-in, and we taxied out into the elements—the rain continuing to beat down on us. It was miserable weather. After a quick check at the end of the runway, we were ready for launch. Since the weather was overcast with a ceiling of 800 feet, we planned to space our takeoff roll to 20-second intervals and use the onboard radar to help maintain separation while in the clouds.

I watched the lead aircraft release brakes and start rolling down the runway. His afterburner kicked in, and a blue orange flame leapt from the rear of the aircraft. Twenty seconds later, the number two aircraft began to roll. As the fifth aircraft in the series, I watched four aircraft become airborne, suck up their gear, and quickly disappear into the dark, gray clouds.

It was my turn to go. I released the brakes, shoved the throttle up into the afterburner, checked my engine instruments, and watched the rain start to roll off the canopy. Once airborne, I raised the gear, double-checked to make sure they were all up, and then fixed my cross check on the instruments just prior to entering the weather. I bumped my radar down to a 20-mile scope and waited to get radar returns from the four preceding aircraft. The departure required a straight-ahead climb for ten miles, so I expected to see all the radar contacts lined up in a row with about two miles of spacing. What I saw was anything but that: the lead aircraft was about 30 degrees left on my scope, apparently in a left turn; the second and third aircraft were flying straight ahead; and the fourth aircraft appeared to be in a shallow right turn.

I asked Lead if he was having problems with the departure, and he responded with a "standby." After several seconds, he then responded with a call, "Don't follow me! I flew the wrong departure!" What a beginning! We were about to fly a 2,000-mile journey, and we couldn't even get the first ten miles right. After a few minutes, we all got back on course and proceeded to our first navigation point over Belgium.

About the time we crossed the German/Belgian border, we broke out of the weather. It was clear and sunny above us. A beautiful white blanket covered the European continent for as far as I could see. It was a spectacular view!

As I was enjoying the sight, relaxing in the notion that everything had settled down, I did a quick fuel check. I immediately discovered that my right external fuel tank was not feeding. I knew that an uncorrectable fuel problem would scrub my mission, and I would be forced to return to the base at Spangdahlem. The thought of turning around was unacceptable. Before informing my flight-lead of the situation, I decided to give myself a few minutes to work the problem. If I couldn't get the tank to start feeding fuel by that time, I would own up to it on the radio and let the flight-lead make the hard decision to turn me around or let me press.

As the time passed, I ran the "Trapped Fuel" checklist several times, trying to get the fuel to feed, but I had zero luck. As I sat there, realizing that my flight over the pond was in jeopardy, I decided to try one last idea. I would change my engine feed knob from the NORMAL setting to the AFT setting and try to "suck" the fuel from the tank. There was no checklist procedure for this, but I knew of no other tricks. I reached down to the left console, twisted the knob to AFT, and stared at the fuel needles. I saw the right fuel needle twitch, and then I saw the needle start to drop. It worked! I was on my way.

Our formation leveled off at 23,000 feet and after passing Belgium, we took a turn to the northwest toward the English coast. We cruised over England and then made a westerly turn out over the Atlantic. With over 100 knots of headwind on our nose, I knew this was going to be a long flight. Our flight plan route called for our first tanker rendezvous at just over 50 miles off the coast of England. Each aircraft in the formation would air-to-air refuel in order to have enough fuel to make Iceland in the event something went amiss during the flight. Passing over the top of England, the weather broke beneath us and I could see the ground.

The tanker rendezvous was picture perfect, and I topped off my aircraft. A full fuel load on the F-16 consisted of about 12,000 pounds of JP-8. It was a comfortable feeling knowing I had a "full tank of gas," as nothing but a watery expanse spread westward. Over the course of the flight, I would refuel seven additional times, always keeping enough gas to divert if the need arose.

Between refuelings, we would spread the formation out and relax a bit. It was at this time that I engaged the autopilot, popped open a soda, and read the newspaper. Every 30 seconds or so, I'd swing my gaze to the side to make sure my wingman was still with me. We were all a bit tired, and the last thing we wanted to face was the prospect of a pilot who fell asleep and slipped unnoticed out of the formation.

As the formation progressed westward, I saw icebergs floating silently in the cold ocean below. Although we had talked about the possibility of having to eject and survive in the ocean, the thought of actually having to endure something like that was a very sobering notion.

At about the eight-hour point, the anticipation of landing in New York began to ease the minor body aches associated with being strapped to an ejection seat for an extended period. My neck was chafed as the rubber lining of the poopy-suit wore an abrasion on my skin.

We refueled for the final time about 300 miles from our destination, an Air Force base in upstate New York, and pushed the throttles up to fly at a faster airspeed. We were flying under rules that dictated that our landing had to be made during daylight hours. With a 10-hour flight behind us, we knew that we would arrive just as the sun fell below the horizon. The flight-lead led the descent, and we spaced ourselves out to a single-file formation to land out of a straight-in approach.

I worked my way to a short final, lowered the gear, and checked for three down and locked. With good gear indications, I flew my jet to a landing just as the airfield lighting popped on. As I taxied my aircraft towards parking, I took a moment to realize that I had "done it." I'd just completed my first flight across the ocean in a fighter. Although tired, I was giddy with excitement.

I thought of my dad, who so many years ago accomplished a similar flight. I felt a nostalgic sense of connection to his aviation achievements. Just as any pilot can relate to another pilot's first solo, I could now relate to all fighter pilots who have flown their aircraft across an ocean. Although I was fully aware that my future in aviation would undoubtedly present more challenging problems than a "pond crossing," I felt the pride and satisfaction of knowing that I had done something that was extremely unique—something that I would remember for the rest of my life.

Reaching "The Big Time"
Tom Poberezny

While attending Northwestern University, I became interested in aerobatic competition. Pilot L. Paul Soucy had two Pitts Specials. His son, Gene, flew the new one (N9J), and I started my aerobatics in the older model (N8J). Under Gene's direction, I learned basic aerobatics and prepared for my first competition in Newnan, Georgia. Unfortunately, when the big day arrived, the competition was rained out!

I finally managed to compete in my first few contests and decided it was something I wanted to actively pursue. I quickly set a goal to become a member of the U.S. Aerobatic Team that would be competing in Salon, France, in 1972. Selections were going to be made at the Oak Grove Airport in Fort Worth, Texas, in the fall of 1971. I only had a few months to enhance my skills from a sportsman competition pilot to the rigors of the "Unlimited" category.

I worked hard and was fortunate to have the support of my family, and most importantly, outstanding mentors such as Gene Soucy and Charlie Hillard. During the summer of 1971, I flew in a few air shows with Gene while practicing for the national competition. Between shows, Gene and I would "live" at the Oak Grove Airport, flying three to four times a day getting ready for the big week of team selection. I was competing against well-known pilots such as Bob Herendeen, Art Scholl, Bill Thomas, and others. Of course, there were "new kids on the block" such as Leo Loudenslager and me.

Finally, after all the practice and hard work, the big day came when we would fly the first of eight flights that would determine the five members of the men's 1972 U.S. National Aerobatic Team. I still remember the nervousness I felt as I strapped into the tiny red biplane, realizing that this was now "the Big Time!" I took off and flew to a pre-designated area, waiting for my turn to enter the aerobatic box. On that day, it looked extremely small.

During the first sequence, there was a series of back-to-back maneuvers that I'd had trouble with in practice because I would "gray out" (not quite go to sleep, but pretty close). I was ready and determined that it was not going to happen to me this time. If I could get through the maneuvers, I knew I would be in good shape.

I entered the aerobatic box and performed the first few maneuvers, when I came to that fateful part of the sequence. I was ready … at least I thought I was. I executed the maneuvers, and all I remember is everything going gray. When I "woke up," I had flown out of the box and "zeroed" the maneuver. I had enough presence of mind to complete the sequence before I landed. I thought I was "cooked." Here I was, a rookie with minimal experience, getting off to a terrible start.

Fortunately, the coaching support I received allowed me to keep a positive presence of mind during the next three flights. By the end of the fourth competition flight, I had placed in the top five. Since the selection process required us to repeat the first four flights. I had to face that fateful sequence again. This time, I made it through the difficult part and went on to become a proud member of the U.S. Aerobatic Team.

Charlie, Gene, and I won the 1972 World Aerobatic Team Championship and ultimately became the Red Devils and The Eagles Aerobatic Team.

I often think back to that first national competition flight. Had I not persevered, I would never have experienced and enjoyed a successful competition and air show career for the next 25 years.

First Flight in the Douglas Skyraider
Jimmy Doolittle III

It was the spring of 1969, and I was brand-new, wet-behind-the-ears, U.S. Air Force Lieutenant. Twenty-something years old and fresh from jet Undergraduate Pilot Training (UPT), I was perhaps a little too proud of myself at this early stage of my flying career and ready (I thought) to take on any challenge.

Some of my fondest memories during UPT involve my T-37 and T-38 instructors, Harvey Sagler and Rudy Haug. The advanced trainer I had been flying for the six months prior to graduation was a supersonic Northrop T-38 Talon. The T-38 is really neat looking and delightful to fly: agile, fast, and equipped with two very responsive turbojets with afterburners. A little under 12,000 pounds at max takeoff weight, the T-38 is a sleek and shiny, little tricycle-gear rocket with a top speed of about 1.1 Mach. The T-38 is a trainer version of the very successful Northrop F-5A fighter. Everything about the T-38 was "new" in the latter part of the 1960s. It had been carefully engineered to avoid the flying and system management pitfalls of earlier generations of airplanes; yet, it was a challenge for a budding military aviator to "stay-ahead-of-the-airplane." For me, the T-38 was an absolute pilot's dream with no real surprises— compared to what I was about to experience.

The Southeast Asia conflict was in full swing between 1969-70, and I was delighted to be awarded an assignment in a fighter/attack airplane. I was proud that I could do my part fighting the protracted war effort overseas.

Douglas engineering legend, Ed Heinemann, was largely responsible for many great Douglas designs, among them the A-1, A-20, A-26, and Heinemann's hotrod, the A-4 Skyhawk. My first assignment was flying one of Ed's most successful designs, the Douglas A-1 Skyraider. This aircraft first flew in 1944, the year of my birth. Originally built for Navy carrier service, they were resurrected from the "bone yard" for USAF counter-insurgency and special operations missions. The Navy called them AD, "Able Dog," or SPAD, "Single Place Attack Douglas." Redesignated as the A-1 by the Air Force, the Skyraider was a workhorse in both Korea and Southeast Asia. My new unit was part of a special operations wing equipped with a little under a hundred SPADs, in addition to many other prop airplanes such as the C-123K, EC-47, O-2, and OV-10. The unit was located at a Royal Thai Air Force base called Nakhon Phanom (NKP) on the Mekong River in northeast Thailand.

Before taking a new airplane into combat, every military pilot attends a conversion course. Mine was at Hurlburt Field, an Eglin Air Force Base auxiliary field near Fort Walton Beach, Florida. I can recall that time as if it was only a few heartbeats ago. I arrived on a Sunday and eagerly strolled out on the flight line to sneak a peek at a Skyraider, an airplane that I was to fly in combat for the next year but had never seen up close and personal before.

Many first impressions are indelibly imprinted in our memories, and my first impression of this wonderful, old airplane was certainly no exception. I had never stood next to a Skyraider and was absolutely astounded by its size. It was big for a recip (reciprocating-engine) fighter, and big compared to a T-38. A 2,700-horsepower Wright Cyclone with a 13-foot-plus prop powered the Skyraider. There were four 20mm cannons, 15 pylons for external stores, and it grossed out at 25,000 pounds, which is a little more than twice the takeoff weight of the T-38. Both single-seat and side-by-side "fatface" versions of the Skyraider were parked on the Hurlburt ramp. The bottom of the engine ring cowl was about high chinning bar height, and the bottom of the 50-foot wing was about head high for an average-size man at the wing root. This beast sat on conventional "taildragger" landing gear, and the amount of oil that leaked on the airplane and ramp was astounding! No wonder they put a 38-gallon oil tank in the airplane. Reputed to have a bomb load equal or better than a B-17, it was truly an impressive attack airplane. Later I learned that the A-1 Skyraider was among the largest of single-engine airplanes to see production in the thousands.

Following a week of ground training, I noticed my name on the flying schedule with my new flight instructor, Captain Dave Lester. On the appointed morning, we met and began briefing for my first flight in this wonderful old beast. Dave was a serious and graying Air Force officer and veteran of a couple combat tours in the Skyraider. I learned later that he had bailed out of an A-1 in North Vietnam—and this was before the airplane was fitted with an escape system. He was probably pushing 30, and I can recall how old (I thought) Dave looked (smile Dave) as he explained the unique starting procedures for the big radial and the traffic pattern/approach techniques for landing the airplane. Of course, I'd have to learn to take off and land a big taildragger before I could be taught air to ground gunnery.

We strapped into a Skyraider, set up the switches and controls for start, and gave the crew chief the hand signal for engine start. I pushed the starter button; the crew chief counted sixteen blades on the big Aeroproducts propeller and gave a thumbs-up. I turned on the mags, waited a moment, and then pressed the primer button next to the starter. If luck was with me, the engine would cough and sputter to life with an immense noise and cloud of blue smoke from the short stacks just outside the cockpit—it did!

But wait, we're not done. The engine was running on the primer fuel flow and the throttle lever was controlling rich or lean. I adjusted the throttle a tiny bit to get the engine running smoothly on primer, then brought the mixture lever to full rich. When the mixture was a little too rich for combustion, the engine stumbled, and as briefed, I took my finger off the primer. Any bit of a false move on the throttle during or before the start would cause a backfire requiring an inlet inspection, and of course, a case of beer for your grinning crew chief. (In the T-38 the start drill was: push a start button, move the throttle to idle—period!) Since my recip engine flying experience to date was limited to tricycle-gear Cessnas and Pipers, about 180 horsepower, I wasn't surprised that my first trip in the Skyraider wasn't pretty.

Dave must have been a patient man! I don't recall him ever asking if I had had any taildragger experience before our first flight, but my lack of tailwheel time was obvious as soon as we finished the post-start checks and began to taxi. It was not a pretty sight. Fortunately, the A-1 has a locking tailwheel option that keeps the taxi mostly straight on the parallel taxiway. Of course, the tailwheel has to be unlocked before, and relocked following, each turn during taxi. (Note: DON'T forget and become airborne with the tailwheel unlocked—the takeoff will likely be OK, but the landing WON'T be fun.)

Arriving at the runway, we accomplished a run-up and checklist typical of most recips and were given takeoff clearance: unlock the tailwheel, line up on the runway, relock the tailwheel and tap a brake to verify the tailwheel is locked, stop and hold the brakes, stick full aft to keep it from nosing over, and gently advance the throttle on the big supercharged radial engine about halfway to around 30 inches of manifold pressure. A quick check of the engine instruments and we were off! Release brakes and begin to gently add power with a target of 56 inches. Then fun begins: Whoa! This airplane really needs a lot of right rudder! I have nearly full right rudder in, and I'm only about two-thirds of target takeoff power. The stick comes forward to lift the tail. Dave is "helping me out" a lot, my heart rate is about a million beats per minute, and as the airspeed builds, I get enough rudder power to get the rest of the power in.

A gentle pull on the stick, and the beast is airborne. Gear and flaps up, pull the throttle back to about 46 inches, pull the prop back to 2,600, and climb out to the practice area for a little air work to try and become a little more familiar with this great old airplane. Power off, she stalls in a rather benign fashion, mostly straight ahead, but power on stalls—WOW! Little or no stall warning in the landing configuration and the A-1 drops a wing to 60 degrees of bank or more in about a half-second. (Note to self: this would be *bad* if I were close to the ground!) Of course, a badly executed stall recovery would lead to a snap-spin encounter—without timely rudder input. The big prop not only generates immense thrust, but a lot of yaw and roll. Lesson learned: every time you move the throttle, you need to do something (the right thing) with your feet on the rudder pedals. So far on this flight, I've not seen *anything* that even a tiny bit resembles T-38 behaviors.

Back in the traffic pattern, the fun *really* begins. We do a couple of stop-and-go patterns and landings with the comical bouncing and directional weaving of a novice taildragger pilot. I'm not thinking it's so comical, and Dave is "helping me" a lot with directional control (sound familiar?). We practice normal patterns and practice some intentional waveoffs. Dave is very quick to point out that I need only a tiny bit of throttle, maybe an inch or two of the 10 inches of full-throttle travel, to accomplish a go-around in the A-1. Dave reminds me that large throttle bursts at slow speeds close to the ground will put you into the ground, upside-down, off the left side of the runway quicker than a blink of the eye—I believe him! Torque roll is what it's called, and I pay close attention to Dave's counsel.

Becoming more comfortable with the Skyraider toward the end of this instructional ride, I begin to relax just a little. Dave knows that my recent experience is in jets with little or no power plant management skills required, so he has me leaning the big radial in the traffic pattern. Not a full-blown manual lean using the torque meter, just a little cruise power-setting exercise: set about 30 inches of manifold pressure, pull the prop back to cruise at 2,200 RPM, and slide the mixture into "normal" for the practice. Dave seems marginally pleased with my progress flying the Skyraider, and we both begin to relax a little more and enjoy the beautiful summer morning here above the Florida panhandle.

Relax? Not so fast! Here we are at 1,000 feet above the pines, and the distinctive and authoritative sound of the big Wright Cyclone hitting perfectly on all 18 cylinders goes unmistakably and completely *silent*. The only noise is the slipstream and the wind blasting through the now windmilling 13 1/2-foot propeller. Oops, I've done it now! The detents in the mixture control in this old SPAD, manufactured when I was about six, are very worn and smooth. In a hurry, I miss the "normal" detent, and it slides into "cutoff." Arrrrrgh! I've shut down the only engine in our single-engine airplane, and the silence is *deafening*! "Quick, undo whatever you just did, bonehead," I say to myself.

In a heartbeat, I move the mixture back to rich, the 36 spark plugs are still sparking and the 115/145 avgas is still flowing. The constant speed prop is doing a good job of holding engine RPM despite the fact that now the prop is turning the engine instead of vice versa. The engine catches instantly and roars back to life. The prop does a good job of quickly harnessing a lot of horsepower, preventing an overspeed. Geez, how many cases of beer would an overspeed inspection or engine change cost me? My very patient and unflappable flight instructor, Dave Lester, never said a word or even turned his head to look my way.

We finish the ride, quietly hang up our parachute harnesses in the equipment room, and complete the debrief. I'm expecting the red pencil to come out with a "U" marked as my overall grade. Dave points out some excellent techniques to improve my landings, marks the grade book with a black "S" for satisfactory, smiles, and we go on our way 'til the next time a day or so later. Guess he figured the lesson was learned!

In the weeks to come, Dave patiently taught me the finer points of air-to-ground gunnery. I successfully completed the conversion course, learning more than a little from Dave Lester about flying heavy, single-engine, recip fighter/attack airplanes. The two hundred some-odd combat missions and nearly six hundred combat flying hours in the Skyraider with the Hobos of the 1st Special Operations Squadron at NKP were relatively uneventful. I returned to the good ol' USA in the summer of 1970 and was assigned to fly the T-38 as a UPT Instructor Pilot in Laredo, Texas. I tried hard to emulate the lessons of patience and persistence that I had learned from great instructors like Dave Lester, Harvey Salger, and Rudy Haug. After all … I had finally come full circle.

A Planetary Exploration Mission
Mark Pestana

Journal Entry: NASA Planetary Exploration Mission.
Atmospheric Chemistry Expedition-Day 34

We've just completed another data collection mission. This is our tenth sortie since beginning the expedition on this planet last month. Our craft, a NASA planetary exploration vehicle, is secure in its hangar, sheltered from the harsh environment outside. The ground crew is busy with their postflight checks of our vehicle's systems. There's only one maintenance write-up to work on, a communication network problem on the Mission Director's panel, and that should be fixed in time for our next sortie 15 hours from now.

The science team has a busy night ahead. Besides the usual data reduction and quick-look analysis, engineers and technicians will spend several hours trouble-shooting anomalies in several of the two dozen sensors and data collection systems installed on our craft. Fortunately there are laboratory facilities adjacent to our vehicle. Any science instruments that need to be taken off our craft for maintenance can be efficiently repaired and tested in close proximity. As always, they'll be installed and ready to go by the time our craft is fueled. Preflight inspection is completed, and the flight crew has finished last-minute mission planning. Then we'll begin another eight-hour mission across a vast, unexplored region of the planet. As a NASA research pilot and flight engineer, I look forward to the challenges of flying this craft in adverse conditions, exploring the unknown, and searching for answers that will increase our understanding of our solar system and the universe at large.

It's amazing how much up-front effort has occurred to get to this point. This expedition, led by NASA, has been the result of two years of planning, integration, and testing. It's actually an international collaboration involving several government agencies and educational institutions. The mission managers have had to coordinate among dozens of scientists and engineers to integrate the experiments and develop an expedition plan.

Cargo transports arrived weeks earlier to pre-position spare parts and consumables. Our scientists need various chemicals such as liquid nitrogen to analyze the atmospheric samples we obtain in flight, and it is important that the supplies be in place before the mission begins. Our team is currently in the middle of a two-month expedition primarily devoted to investigating the planet's atmospheric history and the chemical and physical mechanisms that drive the weather and climate.

It's obvious that this planet has experienced some cataclysmic events in its distant past. Today, while flying just 300 meters above the surface, I observed the ancient remnants of volcanoes, eroded long ago by the forces of water and wind. Dust and gas from these extinct volcanoes may be partially responsible for the chemical reactions that influence weather and climate. The scientists onboard our craft are trying to determine a history of climate change and possibly predict what future conditions may affect this world.

Previously, in the 20th century, NASA developed and perfected its ability to explore our solar system with precision. Specialized instruments, sensors, and data collection systems have traveled millions of miles on various spacecraft that were subjected to the temperature extremes and intense radiation encountered in deep space. Despite these bold efforts, researchers had barely scratched the surface of distant worlds. The more they learned, the more questions arose. Thus exploration will continue indefinitely as long as humans strive to seek our destiny. This expedition is a manifestation of humanity's urge to understand our past and predict our future through a greater understanding of the environments that surround us.

It's time for the crew rest period. In 12 hours we'll repeat the process of fine-tuning the mission plan, conducting preflight sensor tests, and briefing the team before another planetary exploration mission takes off. End Journal Entry.

"Reality"

The expedition I describe above is not a prediction of a future possibility. This mission and many more like it have already happened over the past three decades. These missions are flown over the most important planet in our solar system, the earth, and require a concerted effort by NASA's Airborne Earth Science Program, whose members are sometimes required to operate in primitive and isolated regions of our planet.

These planetary exploration sorties took place in the spring of 1999, flown on a specially equipped airplane from locations such as Fiji, Tahiti, and Easter Island, over vast stretches of the South Pacific Ocean. The "unexplored" territory in this scenario is our precious atmosphere, which is being subjected to an onslaught of pollutants originating as far away as Africa and traveling the air currents around the world. (Yes, I did observe the remnants of ancient volcanoes that peek above the surface of the ocean.) Our investigation included analyses to determine the relative contributions from natural sources, such as volcanoes, as well as human-induced sources of pollution.

Several NASA research organizations are usually involved in these missions. The Airborne Science Program I describe is managed and operated by the Dryden Flight Research Center, located at Edwards Air Force Base in California's Mojave Desert. The "craft" in this adventure is a DC-8, a four-engine airliner built by Douglas Aircraft Company in 1972. Rendered surplus in 1986, NASA acquired and modified it to carry science sensors and perform these explorations.

The missions typically involve one of three types of research: meteorology, atmospheric chemistry, and an earth observation program using a Synthetic Aperture Radar, or SAR, which utilizes data for a multitude of projects. These SAR missions, using the same radar technology that mapped Venus through its thick cloud layer, have detected the minute movements in fault lines, the telltale bulging of volcanic mountains, and the changes in barrier island topography following a hurricane in the Gulf of Mexico. As a spin-off involving historians of ancient civilizations, the radar even peered through dense jungle growth to discover ancient Cambodian temples and Central American pyramids. A similar system operated on a space shuttle mission that, penetrating a few inches through the sands of the Arabian Peninsula, found a Biblical Era archeological site.

Along with an eight-member flight crew, about 35 scientists and technicians sit at various equipment racks within the DC-8 "Flying Laboratory." The logistic support that pre-positions spare parts, consumables, and additional personnel is sometimes provided by U.S. Air Force (active and reserve) cargo aircraft, such as the C-141 and C-17. The NASA mission managers, who also serve as DC-8 mission directors during the flights, orchestrate a multitude of science, engineering, technical, and fiscal tasks that integrate the team effort with precision. Many missions are based and flown from the United States, but deployments to foreign locations require additional diplomatic coordination with the U.S. State Department and embassies abroad to ensure the appropriate clearances are obtained.

The Airborne Science Program also operates two ER-2 (Earth Resources) high altitude aircraft. These modified U-2 reconnaissance planes are capable of reaching altitudes of over 70,000 feet, where traces of meteoric dust can be scavenged from the stratosphere, where the chemical compounds that destroy ozone can be collected, and where a "Big Picture" view of a hurricane can be obtained via remote-sensing lasers and radiometers.

The DC-8, a much larger aircraft, can carry some 30,000 pounds of equipment as well as the scientists that design and operate them. Some science instruments, like laser tables with their associated optical telescopes, are so large that no other aircraft devoted to airborne science can carry them. A unique aspect of the DC-8's carrying capacity is its ability to carry many complimentary sensors, each with its specific objective. This total package of sensors offers scientists the ability to obtain large amounts of data on a single mission and simultaneously correlate significant interrelationships among the multitude of measurements. For example, while one set of instruments is measuring ozone concentration at an altitude of

35,000 feet above the Arctic Sea, other sensors can correlate the relative amounts of compounds, made up of carbon, hydrogen, and chlorine, that may be destroying the protective ozone layer. We usually work in tandem with an ER-2 that flies above us at twice our altitude gathering similar data.

The journal entry at the beginning was an actual mission that was flown from northern Sweden, and engaged the talents, efforts, and cooperation of dozens of scientists and flight operations personnel from North America, Europe, Japan, and Russia. Because our flight tracks sometimes crossed near sensitive areas of the Russian and Siberian Arctic, our mission plans had to be pre-approved through daily coordination with the Kremlin in Moscow. Of course, it helped to have a Russian Air Force navigator sitting in the cockpit observer seat, communicating with the air defense sectors on our HF radio, and ensuring that our identity and purpose were understood. This was especially important because it was the first time since May 1, 1960, that a U-2 (NASA ER-2) was flying high above Russia.

My first flight on a DC-8 meteorology mission took off from Patrick Air Force Base, Florida, in the summer of 1998.

There we were, in the midst of a hurricane … at 39,000 feet over the Caribbean Sea, heading toward the center of a hurricane that would soon make landfall on the coast of Central America. As we enter IMC (instrument meteorological conditions) we rely on our weather radar to steer clear of the heaviest precipitation and turbulence that could end our flight abruptly. The DC-8 is outfitted with sensors that measure size and density of water droplets and ice particles, wind speed and direction, and temperature.

Below us, a Lockheed P-3 Orion operated by the National Oceanic and Atmospheric Administration (NOAA) encounters heavy precipitation at 18,000 feet; and below them, a U.S. Air Force Reserve C-130 Hercules bears the brunt of turbulence and wind shear at 10,000 feet above sea level. At nearly twice our altitude, an ER-2, whose critical airspeed envelope "hovers" a few knots below Mach buffet and a few knots above stall, peers down on vast spirals of clouds that stretch to the horizon. In unison, the sensors on these airborne platforms record a time-coordinated, cross-sectional slice of the hurricane. Additionally, during many missions such as these, we time our combined flight paths to coincide with an overpass of a Terra satellite. One of NASA's next-generation orbiting platforms, the Terra continuously collects earth science data. Scientists can use our data to calibrate and validate the information coming from the satellite.

As young aviators, we are taught to avoid potentially life-threatening thunderstorms. Through a greater understanding of the forces at work here, a thorough safety-review process, a suite of sensors and weather radar, and a prenegotiated set of mission rules and guidelines, we minimize the risks while maximizing our capability for the benefit of gaining valuable data.

For the DC-8, the turbulence increases near the eyewall. The gradually building sound of heavy precipitation is heard over the usual background noise generated by an "airliner" in flight. The forward windows appear translucent as *liquid* water, almost slush, smashes against us. The outside air temperature is -60°C. Liquid?! *Superchilled* water, the scientists remind us. The air around us is saturated with moisture. A constant scan of cockpit instruments reveals that the pilot's and copilot's airspeed indicators, both reading about 250 knots just moments ago, are now decreasing, eventually (and of course erroneously) showing zero. We can see over the glare shield that despite the intensely heated elements in the pitot tubes, a fist-sized mass of ice surrounds both of them. Fortunately, our inertial navigation system, coupled with the GPS, confirms that a ground speed does, indeed, exist. After about 30 seconds of this onslaught, the large amounts of moisture, drawn via engine-bleed air ducts to the aircraft pressurization system, begin to freeze valves controlled by the automatic cabin-pressure controller. As cabin pressure starts to decrease, the flight engineer handles a lever that is linked to an outflow valve. Careful movement of the valve position ensures that cabin pressure is maintained within safe limits. Fortunately, we fly through the eyewall in a few minutes and the ride "softens" a bit, but within 30 seconds, the plane has taken an "elevator ride" down about 1,800 feet! After two more eyewall passes, both with similar results that also affect a few of the science sensors, it's time to call the mission off and return to our host airfield in Florida.

On the return leg we encounter "pop-up" thunderstorms, majestic towers that offer opportune researchers a look at isolated cells. While the weather radar shows only a benign "green" mass, indicating the relatively light precipitation near us, a distinct "pop" with an associated "bump" of the aircraft signals a lightning strike. We do a quick scan of instruments and a poll of the crew reveals that a single circuit breaker has tripped. A postflight check of the plane reveals that the static wicks work as advertised. In fact one is completely gone except for the scorched and melted attach point on the trailing edge of the right wing tip. (The subsequent installation of a lightning-revealing stormscope proves its worth.) What about the 18-inch-long crack in the nose radome and the dimples and missing paint around the nose scoops? Hail damage most likely. After a three-day repair period by our expert maintenance crew, we are back in business.

The hurricane we encountered is dissipating over land. Another tropical disturbance is building off the west coast of Africa, the birthplace of hurricanes. In a week or so, after gaining strength from the warm Atlantic and approaching the Caribbean or U.S. coast, it may be the next target of our pursuit for answers to these kinds of questions: "What strength will it be?" "When and where will it make landfall?" and, "How far in advance can an accurate evacuation decision be made?"

Back to Our Original Story

There we were, just 500 feet above the surface of the Pacific Ocean … south of Tahiti and a thousand miles from the nearest continent. In the distance are strings of small islands. Dense tropical foliage engulfs the remnants of ancient volcanoes surrounded by the coral reefs. As we descend from an altitude of 37,000 feet, through the "purest" air on the planet, atmospheric sampling probes collect traces of carbon compounds, the telltale signature of a burning rain forest in Africa or the unchecked industrial pollution from an Asian factory. The probes are sensitive enough to detect the poisonous particulates from a distant volcanic eruption.

After this expedition, the scientists will return to their laboratories to try to interpret the meaning of the data. What causes "global warming?" Is it human-induced or a natural cycle of earth? What are the immediate concerns to life on Earth? Will global or regional climate changes occur? And if so, at what pace? How will these changes affect the biosphere on this planet, the growing and harvesting seasons, and our very way of life?

NASA Airborne Science missions will continue to seek the answers to these questions and perfect the sensors that will eventually travel in earth's orbit ... and beyond, on other planetary exploration missions.

Phirst Phantom Phlight
Jeff Henderson

On a warm, sunny, humid Florida afternoon, I find myself walking on the tarmac of Homestead Air Force Base. I had always dreamt of flying the machine that was waiting for me. Great warriors and aviators such as General Robin Olds, Duke Cunningham, and Chuck DeBelvue had taken this venerable war bird into battle and returned to revel in their success. I had recently earned my coveted silver wings from the United States Air Force and had completed part of the rigorous intermediate training, when I found myself at the door of the *Stingers* Tactical Training Squadron in Homestead, Florida. Parked out on the ramp were the objects of all of my boyhood dreams, 18 battle-proven F-4D Phantom IIs. These were the first version of the F-4s purchased by the Air Force, and I was about to experience the thrill of flying one.

Although F-4s were no longer the fastest or sleekest fighter, I never looked at my F-4 assignment as a failure. In fact, it was quite the opposite. The new electric jets were having difficulties, and I was glad to be flying a dependable plane. After all, I was about to fly a piece of military aviation history. Better yet, some of the men who had made that history were still around.

Within the first six days of reporting to the squadron, I had the basic systems academics and test completed. During the second week, I underwent two normal procedures simulators, followed by one emergency procedures simulator. All of this simulation experience was required before I could be scheduled to fly.

Enter Capt. Richard "Pete" Pederson. On the day of my first flight I met Pete in the assigned briefing room. I was barely able to contain my excitement as we discussed the required systems knowledge and local area procedures. He said that flying the F-4D would feel a lot like the T-38 trainer in which I had just earned my wings. After the briefing, it was time to proceed to the equipment room to retrieve my helmet and g-suit. Following the equipment fitting, we were off to the aircraft. To say I was excited as I walked out to the flight line for the first time is an understatement. Our flight was to be the last of the afternoon and would bring us back to Homestead right before sunset.

I carefully, and with great reverence, conducted my preflight. After all, this company of aging machines had been "downtown" (Hanoi, North Vietnam) and had come home to share their secrets with a new generation of aviators. I was determined to treat her well and learn to master her with care and respect.

I had always enjoyed reading about this aircraft and had many stories living in my imagination. Stories of future air battles with MIGs, evading SAMs, and baiting the enemy into combat. I am awe-struck to be in the presence of such machines. One Phantom had three red stars (three kills) painted on it. I was connecting to my childhood fantasies in a very real way.

During my moment of reflection, Captain Pederson arrived at the aircraft ready to "strap her on" and show me the ropes. He prodded me to, "get this show on the road."

Starting the old gal was a carefully choreographed set of movements that required the pilot to simultaneously flip all of switches and control the throttle. No doubt, the government specifications when this machine was designed, called for anti-ergonomics. Nevertheless, Pete and I prevailed, and we were rewarded with the heavenly sound of two, J-79 turbojet engines responding to my command. We flipped a few more switches and checked the control surfaces. As big as the Phantom is, it is surprising the small amount of control surfaces that can be seen from the front seat. This is where the crew chief and pilot practice a twisted form of sign language. As the saying goes, *this is not your grandfather's T-33*, but somehow I feel I know her already.

After a call to ground control, I taxied out for the last chance inspection before takeoff. The Phantom held no surprises in taxiing and braking. I could not tell that I had changed from a

10,000-pound training machine to a 48,000-pound war bird. After the inspection, I found myself sitting number one for takeoff on runway 26. The sun is heading toward the horizon, and it was time for us to turn these 17,000 pounds of JP-4 (kerosene) into some useful training.

Homestead tower cleared Stinger 66 for takeoff. I taxied onto the runway as my heart rate began to climb. I was about to become one with history. As we stopped in the takeoff position, I reveled in the thought that I was about to fly one of the very machines that I had long admired from the Vietnam Conflict.

With the throttles set at 85 percent (above that the plane would still move despite maximum brake pressure), I scanned the engine instruments one last time. I heard the roar of the powerful turbojet engines heralding the "moment-of-truth." I released the brakes, advanced the throttles forward, outboard one click, and forward into full afterburner. I am rewarded with a push back into my ejection seat by the 38,000-pound thrust of the J-79s. At this speed these powerful turbojet engines drink 28,000 pounds of jet fuel per hour. By the time we hit full "blowers," we are through 90 knots, and in what seemed to be a few seconds, the nose was starting to rise. For the remainder of the takeoff, I held the stick at full aft. Passing 190 knots, Pete and I became airborne, and the gear came up. The flaps were up before we reached 230 knots. At 300 knots, we were out of afterburner, and following a brief call to departure control—we were on our way! What a rush! Thundering over the south Florida landscape in *a war machine*!

Quickly climbing at over 6,000 feet per minute, I am up to 17,000 feet and then cleared to flight level 220. Checking in with Giant Killer Area Control, I am cleared to maneuver. I would like to say that the business of familiarizing yourself with a new airplane is glamorous, but it is not. However, the stalls, steep turns, slow flight, aerobatics, and so forth were quite predictable, given that in these maneuvers it flew like the T-38. The Phantom does suffer from one weakness. If you exceed 30 units angle of attack (AOA), the airflow blanks out over the vertical stabilizer by the fuselage. The plane departs controlled flight and will try to enter a spin. I was successful in maneuvering near, but not crossing, that limitation.

Time flies when you're have fun! Unfortunately, after a quick glance at my fuel gauge I realized it was time to turn for home. I said "adios" to Giant Killer, and then headed for Homestead. I'm sure glad Pete knew the way. In fact, he wanted to show me the first pattern and landing.

The sun was just about to reach the horizon and of all things, the fiery orange ball was off the far end of the runway. Thundering back into the pattern at 480 knots, horizon ablaze with the setting sun, Pete brought the old gal down on to initial. He told me a list of items to look for as we reached the approach end of the runway. Pete made the four "g" break over the numbers for the final turn. Extending gear and lowering flaps, slowing the airspeed to 180 knots, we were now on downwind. Pete begins the final turn for landing. About halfway around the turn to final, I heard Pete declare that he cannot see anything. The sun was shining in his eyes, and he had poor forward visibility from the back seat.

"Jeff, you've got the plane, buddy."

Heart racing, I was thrust from student/spectator back into the role of pilot. "Roger, I've got the aircraft," I calmly respond as I begin to maneuver the "T-38- like" fighter through the rest of the sinking and turning, visual pattern to the runway. I am sure Pete was making a lot of verbal input to my control, but in that moment, I knew this machine, the one that had returned many an aviator home from combat, would bring me down as well. I touch down and apply full power to make a touch and go. WOW! What an experience!

I will always love and revere "Double Ugly" for its reliability and toughness. I trained and flew in subsequent versions of the F-4 and never feared the newer, more sophisticated jets. I know one thing that all fighter pilots know: it is the man, not the machine that fights. However, when that man is one with his machine, then they are virtually invincible.

Flying the Bell 47
John Boyle

Part I, A Novice's View

I should explain, in case you're a few years younger than I am, that *Whirlybirds* was a popular television series about a pair of guys who operated a helicopter charter service. Every week they found themselves rescuing people, catching crooks, and riding to the rescue—always in the nick of time. Though it sounds pretty corny now, this was when *any* helicopter was a novelty. The series was produced in the late 1950s and seen around the world for years. That is until a sad day when kids demanded shows in color, and to be interesting, helicopters had to be turbine powered and better armed than the 8th Air Force. My love affair with the Bell 47 dates back to watching *Whirlybirds* as a boy. In my case, that affair would date back when the 47 was still in production as the standard civilian helicopter. Growing up on a air force base, the first helicopter I ever saw was a rescue Sikorsky H-19. But from the TV, I knew which helicopter I wanted to fly someday—the 47G. Just like my celluloid heroes, P.T. and Chuck.

It wasn't until the mid 1970s when I actually flew in a helicopter, a Bell Twin Huey. A few months later, my hometown hosted a World's Fair, and I took a couple sightseeing rides in a four seat 47J Ranger. Needless to say, I was more interested in the ride than the sights.

Fast forward through college, career, marriage, you know—general life experiences. I knew that someday I would fly a "Bubble" 47. My determination wasn't without its doubts, for by then a generation or two of machines had superseded the 47. I was told that they were hard to come by, and when you did find one, they were expensive to operate and parts were scarce. Meanwhile, I was able to spend time as a passenger in Jet Rangers and various Sikorskys.

Finally at the dawn of the 1990s, midway through my fourth decade, I finally got a chance to fly in a "Bubble" 47. I stumbled on a training operation in a distant town where 47s weren't seen as unreliable antiques but as hardworking classics still able to earn a living by teaching newcomers about the wonders and demands of helicopter flight. I was busy that day, so I'd have to come back to fly.

A subsequent visit to the city led me to brave a 90-minute drive over the world's busiest roadways to finally fulfill my lifelong dream. I spent the morning waiting for my appointment by looking at an air museum and trying my best to keep my excitement under control. At last, the brown 47D landed and a student exited the left seat.

The instructor motioned me toward the machine. Finally! I had waited 35 years for this moment. I crouched and ran toward the door-less cabin. In my mind I pictured P.T. and Chuck, for they had done this same thing countless times on television. They had done it so often that I figured all helicopter pilots had to learn to run while crouching.

I sat down, buckled my seat belt, and did my best to look rather nonchalant. I wondered what would the instructor think of a grown man stammering like a kid about flying in a helicopter. After all, I was four years older than he was. Over the din of the engine, I put on the headset and had a brief introduction. Finally, the engine noise reached its peak, and the ship began to rise. I was finally flying in a 47!

Once safely at altitude, the instructor asked me to take the cyclic. From years of reading, I knew not to make large hand movements, but I was surprised that it wasn't as tough as I thought it would be. My fixed-wing flight experience was enough for me to gently maneuver the ship. Not forgetting the significance of the occasion, I pulled out a pocket camera and took aerial photos of the surrounding freeway-covered countryside.

We landed after a half-hour. I wanted to stay, but the realities of my life (like living several hundred miles away) made me wonder if I would fly a 47 again.

Part II, The Bell Also Rises

A few months later, I was transferred to a city in the Midwest. Although, my job kept me busy, it allowed me to afford a couple of days each month of having a twin-engine turbine helicopter (and crew) at my disposal. Not a bad deal. Once while flying in the turbine, I saw a red 47 on the ground. It reminded me of my true helicopter love, and I forgot all about the multimillion-dollar machine I was flying.

A couple of years later, I attended a local airshow. Parked off to the side of the displays, I saw something that interested me more than the Thunderbirds and their F-16s ... a *beautiful* 47G-2. I learned that a charter firm had just started up at the suburban airport. A few weeks later, I went out for an introductory half-hour lesson.

After the instructor showed the panel to me and explained the starting procedure, we lifted up, and he took us to altitude. He asked if I had any helicopter time. I said I did, so he gave me the cyclic. Again, it was deceptively easy to maneuver. As the time ran out, we headed back to the airport. I didn't realize my newfound aerial confidence was about to be cut down to size. The pilot hover-taxied us to the grass along the runway, and once in a steady hover, he asked if I wanted to try hovering. I had heard that it was one of the tougher things to learn, but I figured, given the ease with which I had flown at altitude, I was a *natural*! I took the cyclic and made a conscious effort to keep from moving it. Instantaneously, the ground started rushing by. Not only was I moving, but I was flying backwards and to the side simultaneously. Chastened by my impromptu low-level aerobatics, I tried again ... and again ... and again. I went home that day with my old beliefs reinforced: helicopter flying is best done by people whose coordination is better than mine. After all, I didn't learn to ride a two-wheeler until embarrassingly late.

A second, this time full-length, lesson a couple of weeks later reconfirmed my suspicions that I was a klutz when it came to hovering. The aerial work was fine, but when I got close to the ground, the helicopter was like a horse with a mind of its own. Again, I was transferred. I wasn't sure when, or if, I'd fly a 47 again. I hated to quit before I mastered the machine, because if I quit now, I would be convinced forever that I didn't have the makings of another P.T. or Chuck.

Part III, For Whom the Bell Tolls ... About $3 a Minute

A year after I moved to my new locale, I brought the Sunday morning paper home. Looking through the classified ads for sports cars, I stumbled on the aviation section. The "For Sale" ads were limited to a couple of Cessnas and an expensive Bonanza. Under the heading "Aviation Services, Instruction," I saw the ad that would change my life: "Helicopter Instruction ... Bell 47 ... Learn to fly in the helicopter that set the industry standard."

A couple of weeks later, I made a 45-minute drive to a small, suburban field. The helicopter had started life as a Korean War vintage Army H-13E (47D-1), but was later remanufactured into the 47G. The instructor, Jerry, was a man of indeterminate age who looked like a young Ernest Hemmingway. Like his literary counterpart, Jerry had a taste for adventure. He had already survived 2000 instructor hours in a tiny Robinson R-22.

We hit it off immediately. Jerry was cautious, and I liked that. Equally important, he loved the Bell. He felt it was a great trainer because of its high-energy rotor system and gentle characteristics.

Years of reading about helicopters had prepared me for the necessary, and inevitable physics lesson. To sum it up in one word: torque. In order to keep the ship pointed in the right direction, I had to be light on my feet with the antitorque pedals whenever I applied or reduced power. Add power: left foot. Decrease power: right foot.

I also had to know that raising or lowering the collective would change the rotor rpm. To be honest, I didn't realize the importance of the rotor speed needle on the tachometer. I learned quickly that losing too much rotor speed would be as deadly in a helicopter as losing too much airspeed (leading to a stall) in a fixed-wing aircraft. In all my hours in the 47, I spent more time looking at the rotor tach than any other instrument.

On our first lesson, Jerry showed me the preflight procedure. To begin with, climb on top of the center section to check the rotor head and stabilizer bars (it pays to be thin). Check oil and hydraulic fluids. Drain some fuel to check for water. Examine the stabilizer and tail rotor control wires that extend the length of the tail boom. Check the tail rotor gearbox oil. Check the tail rotor blades for cracks and nicks. Examine the right side of the tail boom, the engine mounts, and all the exposed bolts around the engine. Finally, check the cabin and fuel level.

Over the next few months, the starting ritual would become as familiar as starting my car: Mixture - rich; Carb Heat - off; Prime engine open and close; Cycle throttle 2 1/2 times, leaving it a bit open; Battery - on; Switch - on; Step on floor starter; Twist the hand throttle, being careful not to over-rev the engine. Let it warm up until temperatures are good. Check magnetos. Slowly increase throttle to 3,000 rpm (firmly keeping the collective down). Test the clutch by rapidly closing the throttle to split the engine and rotor tach needles. Make sure collective and cyclic control friction is off. Slowly bring power to 3,200 rpm, come on with some right pedal. Slowly the helicopter becomes light on its skids. Before you know it, you're flying. This, along with learning radio and airfield traffic procedures, kept me pretty busy during the first few lessons.

After I learned to control the ship at altitude, the dreaded hover would again prove to be my most difficult lesson. Keeping a more or less straight heading down the runway on departure was easy. Even gradually reducing altitude and bringing it to the proximity of the desired landing area was fine. It was when I tried to hover, to nudge it in the direction I wanted to go, that it would start to meander in some unwanted direction like a wayward horse.

We spent hours in the field across from the fuel pumps, out where some Cessnas and Pipers were tied down. At first, I feared running into them. Eventually I learned to control the 47, so as not to alarm Jerry, myself, or various aviation insurance agents. After five hours, my logbook read, "HOVER!"

After that, the lessons boiled down to a routine: some time hovering and the rest of the hour doing takeoffs, approaches, and landings; either at the airport or a convenient large field a mile south of the airport. The patterns were simple: lift off the dolly, nudge the ship toward the runway (after checking for traffic and making a radio call on the UNICOM), speed down the runway at 60, and let the helicopter fly itself off the deck. Upon reaching 400 feet (over the horse stable), we began a gentle turn to the right. (At our uncontrolled field, helicopters had a right-hand traffic pattern; fixed-wingers, a left.) On the downwind leg, we climbed to 750 feet, and over the eastern end of the airport, turned toward the base and began to gradually lose altitude. When we were nearly lined up with the end of the runway, turn final and keep 600 feet over the big string of power lines inconveniently placed at the end of the runway. Then more altitude, gradually slowing down. Ideally, we ran out of altitude and speed at the same time. Rarely did it work out that easily. The 47 loves to fly. Sometimes, I had trouble getting it down. The broad blades love to produce lift.

More hours passed practicing hovering and patterns. Jerry's voice was heard less frequently over the intercom. He'd let me start the machine. He'd say, "Pretend I'm not here," and I would start the trusty Franklin, run the checklist, do radio calls on the UNICOM, take a final glance, and scoot down the strip. Hovering became less of an event. Finally, I felt like I had real control over the machine.

We practiced recovery from low RPMs, how to slow down from high-speed flight (a relative term in the 47), air maneuvers, and of course, the dreaded autorotation. Getting the machine to autorotate is easy. *Immediately* lower the collective, get the attitude, and keep the speed up. At 50 feet: begin to flare—but don't pull the collective (and heaven knows you want to with the unobstructed view of the earth rushing up to meet you). Level the skids at ten feet, and as the 47 begins to settle, raise *the collective*. By raising the collective at the last moment, the change in blade pitch gives you a nice cushioned landing. Easy really, especially if you have calm nerves and good reflexes, neither of which are strong points of mine. The autos went fairly well; except for the one time I flared too steeply and scraped the tail rotor guard on the pavement.

Finally the day came. We were out by the Cessnas, and Jerry had me land from a typical low hover. Only this time, he said he was getting out. So as I held the collective down firmly, he undid his seat belt and stepped onto the grass. Moving 30 feet in front of the helicopter, he signaled me to rise. Without much fanfare (except in my mind), I was flying solo. Okay, the altitude was three feet, and my instructor was within running distance, but I was flying an aircraft with nobody beside me.

Six more hours passed with much of the time-spent solo.

In the low winter light, I could often see my shadow on the ground; clearly seeing through the bubble that I was, in fact, alone.

One day I arrived at the field, and in our preflight conference, Jerry announced that if a couple of patterns went as well as he thought they would, I could really solo—fly around the pattern.

The patterns went well ... 60 ... stable ... turn ... climb downwind ... turn base ... lose altitude ... final ... wires ... landing. I knew the procedure cold. He had me hover to the parking area and land. He got out and told me to fly the pattern. I was too busy thinking to be nervous. When I was up, I looked to my right to scan for traffic. Only then did I notice the empty bench beside me. I let out a laugh and thought, "You are really up here by yourself. Neat!!!" The flight ended uneventfully. I was finally a helicopter pilot.

Subsequent flights had me go further afield by myself, and I began to practice cross-countries. I'd fly to a nearby suburb, staying away from the homes, always looking for potential emergency landing spots (the ball fields, parks, and mall parking lots were welcome sights). For my first solo trip to the suburb, I had studiously figured a compass course during flight planning and confidently followed my heading. When I expected to be over the town, nothing looked familiar. I had a hunch I was too far west, so I backtracked over the main road. Finally, I saw my primary landmark—a large church steeple. I was thankful I didn't have to call Jerry for help, or worse, land to find out where I was.

On a dual cross-country, we flew to a small field frequented by ultralights, homebuilts, and a Cub or two. They were having a fly-in, and we were the hit of the show. I have to admit it was an ego-enhancing experience to land the 47 (with every eye in the place watching) and casually get out, like I was parking a car.

Our farthest cross-county was the best yet, across a wide river (I wonder what ditching the thing would be like) and finally finding the grass airfield alongside the railroad track just outside of town. A bit of gas and a soda, and we were on our way. It was a beautiful summer day. The countryside was warm and green. I was relaxed enough to watch the world go by (always keeping one eye on the rotor tach) and really enjoy the scenery.

Unfortunately, it was to be my last ride with Jerry and my beloved Bell. Two days later, on a new student's first flight, the transmission failed. Jerry autorotated in a field. (I knew it well; I had often practiced above it. The nearby farmhouse had brown trim and a shed out back.) He called the airport, and they collected the stricken chopper the next day with a trailer.

"The student took it very well. He had the controls when I heard the strange noise, felt the RPMs drop off. He didn't panic, I just took the controls and landed," Jerry calmly explained. I could see it in my mind's eye, because I had run through similar scenarios in my own mind countless times. I'm glad the student didn't scream or freeze, but I wondered if he'd ever come back for his next lesson.

Well, the Bell would be down for a while, a long while. The transmission had less than 200 hours on it since being rebuilt. Lawsuits were threatened. The 47 wasn't going anywhere soon.

Unfortunately, I was. I had been transferred yet again. So here I was, almost two years later, and still only hours from getting my ticket. And not a 47 school within 400 miles. There was an R22 school about four hours away, but they required students to have 20 hours dual before solo. I might as well started over.

So it's either wait to fly again until I could spend a few weeks away, or buy one. I scanned *Trade-a-Plane* and looked at my funds. My mind races … a neighbor flies the medical Long Ranger in town, and one of his staff pilots has a CFI. My friends at a local television station have said if there would be a chopper in town, they would guarantee a few hours a month as a news ship, but this town is too small for traffic reports.

Why the helicopter might pay for itself!!! Optimism runs rampant, but fiscal caution prevails. For now.

One thing is certain: I'm not done with 47s yet!

The Day the Sky Fell
Judy Rice

Tuesday, September 11, 2001, 6:00 A.M.

Beautiful day! All set to go fly. Grumman was topped off yesterday for an early departure today. A call to flight service reported "patchy fog along route of flight … temperatures and dew point spread …" Only one-degree spread, so I have another espresso and wait an hour for the fog to burn off. Better to be safe and wait a bit than the ole' saying of wishing on the ground.

7:00 A.M. At The Hangar

Preflight on a cool fall day in Oshkosh, Wisconsin is a pleasant experience. My almost finished, beautifully painted Grumman is ready to go. Today I return the Grumman to Kenosha, Wisconsin, to finish the detailing. Earlier, I had anxiously borrowed the Grumman before the paint shop had completed the final details.

Pulling the Grumman out of the hangar is never an issue. But today, his right main will not go up over the pestering cement lip that meets hangar to ramp. Grummans are known for a stubborn castering nose wheel on pushback, but this is the first time in five years of ownership that I have had difficulty pulling him out of the hangar. I wonder if the Grumman knows something that I don't. The fog has burned off, and winds are light; preflight and run-up—all in check. Time to go, Grumman!

8:00 A.M. Wheels Up

A southerly turn indicates clear skies all the way to Milwaukee. I can almost see the skyline as I roll out on heading. Fifteen miles south of Fond du Lac, I reach 3,500 feet and level off. Winds at altitude are 225 at six knots; I can't ask for much more. I request an MKE flight following and am given the required transponder code to dial in. ATC states, "Radar contact."

Ten miles north of Kenosha, I am handed off to Center. I dial in number 2 radio to Kenosha ATIS keeping the second ear for any center advisories. Kilo ATIS is calling for light winds, runway two-four. Airport is in sight just as ATIS switches to Lima, "Kenosha Airport is closed to all IFR/VFR traffic."

I said out loud to the Grumman, "That is it? WOW, must have been some bad accident, with two parallels and one crossing, to close all runways."

I reach for the Jepp Guide to check out Racine runway configurations. I'll sort this out when I'm on the ground. Within seconds, Center states, "All IFR/VFR traffic has been canceled."

I say to the Grumman, "What the hell does that mean?"

The controller continues, "AIRMET in effect; National Emergency in effect; All IFR/VFR traffic is to land at the nearest airport."

I scream to the Grumman, "WE HAVE BEEN NUKED! OH MY GOD; WE HAVE BEEN NUKED!" I am sure it is Chicago, barely 25 miles to the southwest. Goose bumps and dazed.

The radio comes alive. American … United … NWA … all the heavies, asking the controller what seems to be all at once, "We have been cleared … What do you … I'm IFR!"

The controller replies within seconds, "*Shut up*! No more questions. This is a *National Emergency*. I will call you individually by tail number, *and* you will land at the airport. I state—if you do not, you will be shot down."

I listen, stunned. Unbelievable! I cannot even imagine what is happening down there. All I can do is fly the airplane. I listen carefully for "Grumman 6300L." I hear vectors being given to

Madison, Green Bay, or Waukesha. What will I find when I'm permitted to land; where will I be permitted to land, and when?

To my surprise, after what seems like endless time, I hear, "Grumman 6300L, you are cleared to land at Kenosha." I pause, as if I did not hear correctly. I repeat, and the controller repeats, just as I had, in fact, heard. Wheels down. Rollout. I did not know what to expect. Guns? Devastation? What? Ground control clears me to paint shop. In the short time I have known William, the painter, he has always worn a smile. I taxi up to his grim face, head bent close to the radio.

Today the sky fell.

THE HOMEBUILT

To invent an airplane is nothing. To build one is something.
To fly is everything.
-Otto Lilienthal, pioneer aircraft builder

The Flying Flivver
Verne Reynolds

You see, I had this Uncle Elmo. Some folks called him a "cut up," but to me, he was just plain Uncle Elmo. I always thought he was kind of fun to be around because you never knew what he was going to come up with next. He'd try most anything at least once, and maybe twice if he didn't quite get the hang of it the first time. So it wasn't much of a surprise when one day he said he thought he'd build himself an "airy-o-plane" and teach himself how to fly in it, too.

He'd seen a picture of a real early airplane that came out in a *Popular Mechanics* magazine that summer (in the early 1930s—maybe 1931 or '32) and that's what made him decide he could build one. Because after all, it didn't look all that complicated. And he knew that some fella named Lindbergh had flown his plane clear across the ocean, so he *knew* they were perfectly safe to fly.

He went out to the barn and started sawing out some pieces of wood and nailing them together, and before long, by golly, he had made a pretty good start. He already had an old Model T engine over there in the corner of the machine shed, and after a spell, he finally got that engine bolted onto the front end of his "airy-o-plane." He started out calling it an "airy-o-plane," but then shortened it down to "airy-plane," and later on started calling it an *aircraft* after so many people said, "What's that thing you buildin' there, Elmo?" *Aircraft* seemed more scientific somehow. People would just sort of stand around slack-jawed when Uncle Elmo said he was going to fly it, too, someday. Then he wrapped some old bed sheets around the wings so's they'd overlap real good and then he stitched them up real good and tight, so's you could drop a quarter on them wings, and the quarter would bounce—sometimes.

He knew he needed a little wheel back there on the tail end, and he was kind of stumped for a while until he remembered he had an old swivel plate off a DeLaval Cream Separator that would be just the right size. And so he bolted that on, sideways, and it worked just fine—it swiveled and everything. He already had the wheels from a busted bicycle that he called "the main gear" 'cause that's what they had called it in *Popular Mechanics* magazine. He had quite a time trying to figure out where to put the propeller. Whether it should go up front by the radiator fan, or in the back by the transmission, but he had bolted the engine on up front by that time. He couldn't put the propeller in back of the engine because that is where he planned to sit. So, it had to go up front. To complicate things, he had to figure out a way to make that propeller spin faster and faster when he wanted it to. Of course he could shift gears with his feet, like he did in the Model T, but how could he get the transmission to drive the propeller? So he thought about it and did some sketches, and then it came to him that he could use a couple of universal joints and some chain from the corn planter to make up a belt system like Charlie had done on his threshing machine. *And* he'd bet anything it would work.

But first off, he needed a propeller. He studied the *Popular Mechanics* magazine some more. Then he took a good stout two-by-six, what was holding up the slack there in the corner of the garage, and he took his draw knife and settled down to whittle a propeller out of solid oak. Took him almost a week before he was satisfied with it, but it was a thing of beauty. Looked just like the one in the magazine, and he thought maybe he ought to take a picture of it and send it to the magazine to show them what he had done. But then he thought he'd wait until he had it all assembled and maybe send them a picture of his *aircraft*. Better yet, he could send a picture of himself flying his own *aircraft*.

So, he bolted his oak propeller onto the front of the engine and connected it to the transmission with his belts and chain and universal joints. And it looked good to Uncle Elmo. He still had to figure out a way to crank the engine. He found out that if he made a real long crank with quite a bend in it that he could flip that engine, and it would almost always catch and start right up. Well, that is if you had the carburetor primed just right. He was so proud of himself he almost asked Aunt Edith to come and take a look at what he was building, but then he remembered she hated to see him wasting time tinkering with stuff out there by the machine shed when he could be fixing screen doors or doing something worth doing.

He had an old kitchen chair that he cut the legs off of to make it into a seat for his *aircraft*, and for a joystick, he used a broom handle that he cut off just the right length so's he could connect it and make the wings go up and down when he wanted them to. Oh, he had it all figured out, and he was so proud. He'd sit in the chair in his flying machine and pretend he was flying and he'd move them wings and everything. And one time the neighbor's dog came over to visit and tried to pee on Uncle Elmo's landing gear and Uncle Elmo liked to had a fit. He scared that dog so bad he never did come back. At least not for that whole summer.

So, Uncle Elmo hand-lettered the word *Experimental* on one side of his airplane and on the other side he hand-lettered the words *Elmo's Flying Flivver*, because he thought that would look kind of pretty. All he had was some leftover red barn paint, and boy did it look nice on that white, bed sheet fabric. Oh! He *was* proud. He was just awful proud of what he had done. All by himself he had built an *aircraft*.

Now I wasn't there, but I do remember him telling me about his first flight. How he took off going downhill between the machine shed and the chicken house, and how tickled he was when he got up enough speed and it actually flew with him in it. He was yelling for Aunt Edith to come and watch him fly! He had his cap turned around backwards and he had goggles and everything, just like he had seen in *Popular Mechanics*. He wanted everybody to see him fly! He wiggled his joystick, and the wings went up and down, and he made some right turns and some left turns in it. And then he flew over his neighbor's barn lot and Charlie, his neighbor, and all the kids came running out and they wanted to see him land that thing. So they piled into Charlie's car and headed over to Uncle Elmo's, which wasn't too far away. But by the time they got there, several other cars were already there, full of people who wanted to see what was going on and what was going to happen, because they could hear the *aircraft* and they could hear Uncle Elmo yelling for Aunt Edith to come and watch him fly.

And then Uncle Elmo flew down pretty low over the chicken house and yelled something else at all the people who were there by now. He scared the chickens so much that they all started to cackle and run around every which way, and the dogs started to bark and chase the chickens. Aunt Edith was fit to be tied because she knew that commotion would throw a bunch of her old hens into what they called "layer's shock" when their rear ends tighten up so much they can't squeeze an egg out. Now while all of this was happening, Uncle Elmo realized he had a problem. He still had to land this thing, and *Popular Mechanics* didn't say anything at all about landing. So he made one pass at the place where he had took off from, there by the machine shed, but there was so many people and so many dogs running around in the dust (not to mention the feathers that were just about everywhere) that Uncle Elmo had the gut feeling he'd never be able to put that aircraft back on the ground in one piece.

So he headed for the straw stack there in the corner of the barn lot where the threshing crew had piled up the straw when they had threshed the oats. He remembered that when he was a kid he had jumped into fresh straw from the haymow door and he hadn't busted anything, so maybe he could just jump out of the *aircraft* into the straw stack and let the plane land itself. That's what he planned to do, all right.

Just as he was about to put his plan into action, he sort of remembered that he had only put one gallon of gas in the tank before he started to fly. So there he was about 50 feet high, pointed straight at the straw stack, and the engine just up and quits. He only had time to yell something that nobody quite understood, and then he flew smack dab into the side of that straw stack.

Which would have been all right, except that quite a few of the chickens had bee-lined it for the straw stack when the dogs were chasing them. Well, when Uncle Elmo and his *aircraft* hit that straw stack, them chickens thought the world had come to an end. They flew out of there in every which direction, screeching their heads off and puckering up so tight half of them would never lay again. Now, the dogs were really barking, and the chickens were making a fuss; and Aunt Edith was yelling for Elmo to stop flying, which he already had, of course. The neighbors were hoping Uncle Elmo was all right and they started clawing away at the stack trying to dig him out. They were hollering his name and diggin' in the straw, it was pretty noisy there for awhile what with the neighbors and the dogs and the chickens and Aunt Edith and everything. About that time, Uncle Elmo walked around to their side of the straw stack and asked them what they were doing. Seems he had gone plumb through that straw pile and tumbled out the other side, good as new. He didn't even have a scratch on him, although he did itch a lot for a couple of days from all the chaff that got down his neck. And he had some nasty chicken stuff all over his shirt and his bib overalls, but outside of that, he was fine.

Oh, he was quite a celebrity. Whenever he went downtown, people would point at him and tell their kids something. And every time he went flying after that, half the town would jump in their cars and race out to Uncle Elmo's barn lot just to see him land his *aircraft*. He never did learn how to land in a pasture or anywhere except that straw stack. After that Aunt Edith always kept the laying hens locked up in the henhouse and made the dogs stay in the basement whenever Uncle Elmo said he thought he'd go fly awhile. She just couldn't stand the thought of losing all those eggs again when she had to set the table with her eggs and cream money.

The rest of that whole summer, Uncle Elmo flew his *Flying Flivver* almost every week when it wasn't raining or time to cut thistles or something. It got so as all the kids in town would bicycle out to the farm and hint real big that maybe Uncle Elmo ought to fly his machine today, but he had a lot of other things to do too. And besides, sometimes he liked to just sit and look at his *aircraft* and smile and hum and think about that first time when he took off there by the machine shed. He was awful proud.

We all were awful proud of him too. But Aunt Edith usually had kind of a hard time admitting it.

Flying the Waco
Paul H. Poberezny

During high school, my Ancient History teacher recognized my total interest in airplanes and not in class work (especially in ancient history). I was not doing well in school. One day he mentioned that he had a damaged Waco. This is a gilder that gets towed into the air behind an automobile and has a frame on which the pilot sits out front. He said he would give it to me if I would repair it. *And* he gave me $67 to cover the costs of dope, fabric, and spruce. I took it out in the country, to the family garage.

I came from a poor family. My dad is from Russia and my mother from Arkansas. While learning how to rebuild the glider, I studied books on how to fly—which way the controls moved, and what they moved (ailerons, elevator, and rudder).

In 1937, after much work, my high school chum Eddie Hoelfer helped me tow it behind his Whippet automobile to a nearby farmer's field. Of course, a bunch of the neighbor farm kids and school kids were there to see my first flight.

We had about 500 feet of rope stretched out and hooked onto the bumper of his little 1932 Coupe. I waved my arms to indicate that I was ready, and he started off. One wing dragged on its skid. I pushed the stick over to the left and the left wing went down. After a few tense moments it finally went back to neutral. The next thing I knew, I was in the air! What a sight! What a thrill to look down from a new dimension. I was sure that I was at least one hundred (it was probably more like twenty-five) feet in the air!

I released the rope and learned an important lesson—keep your nose down. Even with this mistake, I managed to have a pretty solid landing. Several more flights took me to higher altitudes and gave me a better understanding of the controls.

I will always remember the smell of being drug through the alfalfa grass during that first flight. After 30,000 flight hours, and having the privilege to have flown some 400 types of aircraft from military jets to homebuilts—that flight in 1937 is the one flight I will never forget.

A Vari Viggen Story
Ron Smith

It all started a long time ago in a faraway place. (February 1972, Flint, Michigan—college) One day, one of my roommates and I were talking about model airplanes and discovered that both of us had built and flown models in our younger days. I remembered stashing some of the survivors of my brother's and my own exploits in the attic at home before I went to college and readily volunteered them for "service." They were old, and we were rusty, so several disasters soon followed. Before long, we became known as the "Wrong Brothers" around the fraternity.

One day I came across a magazine that caught my attention. It was called *Plane and Pilot*. There was a picture of an American Traveler on the front and an article in it about a Frenchman, Marcel Jurca who was designing and selling plans for replicas of World War II fighters that you could build and fly yourself. I bought the magazine and read the article about ten times—my dream had begun! I announced to anyone that would listen that someday I was going to build an airplane and fly it. Everyone thought I was "nuts," including my new bride Pamela T. Obviously, this was not the time or the place to begin fulfilling such a dream, so it had to "fester" for several years.

To our amazement, Pam discovered that she was pregnant right before I graduated from college. She was delighted, but it was a few years sooner than I had expected. She determined that since she got something she wanted that I should get something I wanted. Much to my delight, it turned out to be flying lessons. She would have gotten pregnant sooner if I had known that!

The lessons were a lot of fun, and I received my license in August of 1974. I was very anxious to demonstrate my new skills, so the first thing on my agenda was to take Pam for a ride. She, however, was not so anxious but eventually agreed to cooperate. Most new passengers want to see something on the ground that they will recognize, and Pam had requested to see her mom and dad's house. No problem! That was the first place to which we flew, and where I proceeded to demonstrate my "turn-about-a-point" skills in about a 45-degree bank. I learned another very important lesson about new passengers when we landed and Pam jumped out of the plane and proceeded to puke all over the ramp. Her limited interest in flying just went negative.

Time went on without much flying, but my dream was still floating around waiting for an opportunity. It presented itself without warning in January of 1975 when my aunt surprised me with a check from my grandmother's estate. Pam and I bought a clock to remember her by and paid some bills. But more importantly, Pam agreed (a little reluctantly) to set aside $1000 to start an airplane. She didn't mention it at the time, which is unusual for her, but she considered it worth the money to get this notion out of my head.

The search was on! I had found a magazine with a summary of homebuilts in it. (Kits were unheard of at the time.) My criteria were simple and naive. A two-place fighter that would be easy to build. Wood was a definite advantage because I didn't know how to weld, didn't have the equipment, and what few attempts I had made at sheet metal were disastrous. Looking through the book, I soon realized that there weren't any two-seat scale fighters. Then, Wow! What's that? There were two people in there, but the tail is in the front! It's made out of wood, and it's OK for a first-time builder. (Ha, like I said, I was naive.) It looked like it could be a fighter, *and* it can be built for about $5000. Including everything! (Double Ha!) An average person could build it in two to three years. (Triple Ha!) It was called a Vari Viggen. Named after a Swedish fighter aircraft with the tail up front. Hey, that's kind of neat. Not being one to belabor decisions, and having had relatively good luck throughout my life with instinctive decisions, a $53.00 check was in the mail to this Rutan guy on January 13, 1975, for a set of plans. I sure hoped that he was honest and didn't skip town with my money.

What made me think I could build this thing? I didn't have a very good answer to that one. Looking back knowing what I know now and what I knew then, I would agree with everyone else and declare myself "nuts." Most of my experience had been tinkering with cars and things around the house. My attitude was, and still is, that if something is broken I probably can't hurt it; so, I would dive in and see what I could find out. This theory generally held with few exceptions, and I learned about a lot of subjects and built-up my confidence experimenting with things that previously I knew nothing about. Also, I find it very difficult to give up on a project once I start. This is probably more of a character flaw than an attribute. From the pictures, this thing looked as if it went together like a big model. And having built quite a few of them, I considered myself a "pro." No problem!

In the meantime, I told everyone I knew about this new venture. Once again, most of them told me that I was "off my rocker." There were, however, a few notable exceptions. One was my old "Wrong" brother from my college days with whom I have always kept in close contact. His real name is Jim Radowski, and he is now finishing his second homebuilt, a modified Laser. He had told me from time to time about this place called Oshkosh and how they put on a heck of an air show once a year. When I told him that my airplane plans were on the way, he once again reminded me about Oshkosh. He said that the group that runs it is called EAA (Experimental Aircraft Association) and that they are into homebuilts big time. He recommended that I join EAA. He wasn't alone. By that time, a few other people had suggested the same thing.

Things were starting to happen very fast, probably the only time during the project that they did. An old check register shows that a check for $879.93 was written on the 1st of February to Wicks Organ Co. for all of the wood that I was going to need. (And it almost was!) I remember driving over to pick it up. Unknown to me, Pam was thinking that this was going to be pretty expensive firewood, but it will get this crazy idea out of his head. On the 16th of the same month, the register shows the most important check ever written from our account concerning aviation. It was for $20.00 to EAA.

Construction

The plans arrived very quickly after being ordered. I remember looking through them and gulping. The magnitude of this project was starting to soak in. There were a lot of things in the plans that I had no idea how to do. I determined that the wood parts were probably the most logical place to start and that we would just grind through this thing one step at a time. Burt suggested starting with the canard so that the builder (me!) could get a feel for how the process would go and be able to bail out with minimal time invested and dollars spent if he/I didn't like it. I, however, decided to start with the fuselage because I already had the wood and didn't know what to do with a canard hanging around, and possibly warping, for who knows how long. (Maybe two or three years—ha!) The jig was built, and away we went.

Pam got used to not having a garage a lot better than I had expected. She was still thinking it would just be a temporary inconvenience until I got over this idea. As the realization began to hit her that this thing wasn't going to go away, I started noticing hints as subtle as her notes saying "Ron, I miss you!" laying on my work bench and as crude as a loud voice and red face ordering me to assist her in some menial domestic task. Still young and naive, I thought these were just "girl things" that I had to put up with.

One day Pam told me that she heard a noise out in the garage. When she went out to investigate she saw the UPS guy laying under *her* airplane. He was just interested in airplanes and recognized it as one! I started to notice that when people were around it was referred to as *her* airplane, and when we were alone it was *my* airplane. I could live with this notion since it represented some degree of support for me. Believe it or not, as things started working and it actually looked like it would fly some day, she began encouraging me to get out in the garage and work on it.

I agree with the person who said that building an airplane is not a big project; it is a whole lot of little ones. When I was able to work a lot of overtime, I would buy parts, and when I wasn't, I would work on them. I was constantly looking for opportunities. One day, a friend at work was looking through the *Trader* and came across an ad for an engine for $500. After a few phone calls to "advisors," I bought the engine.

Whenever I encountered something I didn't know how to do, I would start asking people questions. At times, I would ask the same question to several people, not because I didn't believe the first person, but because in this way I would learn about new things. There were so many talented and knowledgeable people around me that I felt obligated to take in as much information as I could. You have heard it before, and you will hear it again—I could not have even come close to getting the job done without the people in EAA. I don't think there is a finer bunch in aviation than Burt Rutan and his organization. The ideas and help that they provided were invaluable to me. It was blind luck that they were behind the project I had chosen.

The wings of this plane were unlike anything else that I had seen. The original plans called for them to be made out of aluminum. But before I got to them, Burt developed a revolutionary new process called composite construction. (Being slow does have some advantages.) I decided right away that that was the way to go. I was happy to learn that although I did not have any experience with fiberglass several of my aviation friends were experts. Jimmy Dallas arrived on the scene bearing an epoxy pump, squeegees, etc. and Ross Gresley, Mike and Loretta Ludek, and some friends of friends showed up to offer badly needed helping hands. You have to be organized and work fast once you start, and we did. This process consists of four layers on an entire top or bottom wing surface that must be applied simultaneously before the epoxy cures in order to be successful. The first of four lay-up sessions took us six hours, and by the time we did the last one, it took only two. The wings turned out great.

The paint job was the last construction project. From the beginning of this project, I considered it from time to time, but I have never been very good at painting and my chances of coming up with a good scheme were next to nil. One day in passing, I mentioned it to Steve Givens. He said simply, "Bring it over to my place, and I will paint it if you do all of the grunt work." Sounded like a heck of deal. It was also a heck of an education. Part of the prep work was sanding the plane with very, very fine sandpaper. Who would ever have dreamt that you could sand with stuff that fine. As it turned out, several people helped me sand including Steve and Tim Michaels. When the paint job was finished, it turned out better than I could have ever imagined thanks to these talented and generous people.

The airplane was rolled out of the "Givens Paint Works" on October 15, 1989. It was 14 years, 9 months, and 2 days after the plans were ordered. My plane was finally on the way to the airport for final assembly.

Flying

The weeks following the airplane's arrival at the airport were very intense. A lot of finishing touches, weight and balance, getting the FAA to come out, and last but not least, firing up the engine. This is always a milestone, but it was especially one for me because it was the first engine I had ever overhauled! My "coaches" had done well because it fired right up. The only engine-related problem I had was a blown crankshaft seal and a minor carburetor problem. The only other problem I encountered during this time was when the nose wheel collapsed during my first attempt to taxi. It was a major disappointment and embarrassment since there was a bit of a crowd standing around. As it turned out, I had an over-center lock adjusted a little too close to the center, so that when the strut flexed it pushed the lock past center the other way and put the entire load on a 1/16" cable. The cable snapped and down I went. The only damage was the broken cable and a cracked nose cone. The over-center stop was adjusted, the cable was replaced with a 3/32" cable, and it has worked well ever since.

Finally, the day was arriving. The plane was signed off. It had 10 hours plus run time, the nose had been rotated during high-speed taxi, and all kinds of little adjustments had been made. My strategy was simple. I was going to wait for good weather, sneak out unannounced, and go in early in order to avoid the pressures of a big crowd—just like all the articles about first flights said to do. I'm glad that it didn't work out that way. The people around here have developed a sixth sense about these things. Ed Escallon grabbed me the day before I flew and gave me a rundown on first-flight strategies and procedures that were successful for him. This not only helped me refocus from the hustle-and-bustle of getting this thing working to flying, but also gave me valuable information that could have saved my life if an emergency arose. Also, it kept me busy during the flight and helped keep my nerves under control.

When the morning of Sunday, November 12, 1989, rolled around, there was no doubt in anyone's mind that this was it. The day was cool, clear, and best of all, there was no wind! There must have been 20 people there, and they were all very supportive and careful not to exert any pressure. I was glad they were there both before and after the flight, and besides that, we got a lot of great videos and pictures.

The plane was pulled out and fired up. As I was taxiing out, the thought actually crossed my mind, "I wonder if I will still be around tomorrow?" The only time I could remember being that nervous in an airplane was before my first solo flight. Back to business; run it up, go through the checklist and cleared for takeoff. Oh boy, here we go! The plane feels good and is running well.

Ed says, "Fifty feet by the tower or abort." The nose is coming up and we're off. Fifty feet? No problem! The speed is good. The climb seems slow but OK. Where do I go if it quits? Temps, pressures, ailerons working well, slow flight, etc. I don't remember relaxing for one moment during the whole first flight.

It took three attempts to land. The thing didn't seem to want to come down, but when it did, it was a very nice landing. There were a lot of congratulations and hugs from the crowd and even a little impromptu party. I could finally breath easily and savor the moment.

After several flights, I found that I could actually relax and enjoy flying this amazing airplane when *IT* happened. My plane had a total of eight hours on it when I put the landing gear down to land and the main gear transit light stayed on … and on … and on. I looked out to see what was going on. Nothing! A pang of panic ran through my chest. I cycled them a few times, still nothing. I tried some abrupt pitch changes to see if they could be jarred loose and still nothing happened. The tower offered to take a look. He agreed—they were still up. Well, it was time to try the emergency system. I grabbed the tee handle, gave it a pull, and up it came—the *whole thing* right out of the floor. Things were looking bad and besides it was getting dark.

I started to remember having read Rutan's account of his gear up landings. *Thank God* he had pioneered this maneuver. I knew the personal danger was minimum, but there was a good chance that there would be some degree of damage to the airframe if I landed with the main wheels up. The nose wheel was down and locked. The tower offered the grass alongside of the runway. Nope, Rutan used the pavement and so would I. Turning final, I saw the airport fire truck, pickup truck, and jeep sitting on the taxiway. To top it all off, Pam had gotten wind of this and was in the tower "having kittens." Crossing over Highway 32, I shut the engine off to save the prop, and the plane greased right on down. Just like it knew what it was doing. But then I realized that I was headed right for the runway lights. We, the plane and I, were kind of going sideways right off the side of the runway. I stomped on the left rudder and brake while being totally aware that it probably wouldn't do a thing for me, but I knew I couldn't just ride into those lights. Unbelievably, the thing made a nice little "S" turn around one light and ended up stopped halfway off the runway between two runway lights.

I showed the skid marks to everyone out there to reassure myself that I didn't imagine it. It was as plain as day that it had happened. I still can't explain how. The wing tips were not even scratched. The only damage was to the little "grocery cart" wheels under the skids in the back that threw their treads and were ground off and to the skids which were ground down about 1/4". It cost about $15 and two hours to fix the damage. As for the cause, there was no obvious problem. The wheels came right down when it was hoisted up off the ground. I even taxied it back to the hangar. A few adjustments were made, and a new emergency cable (different style) was installed. They and the airplane have worked fine ever since.

This has been a long story, but it was a long project. I hope it was worth waiting for, "Pam's" Vari Viggen was.

The Plane is Ready—Pilot is Not
David McCormick

This is a short account of a first flight in my homebuilt airplane. It took place on June 25, 2001, at Jersey Shore Airport, Pennsylvania.

After four years of building my Kitfox Classic IV, N195CL, I recorded my airworthiness certificate on June 22, 2001. The airplane was ready to FLY but the pilot wasn't. I had not given much thought about flying my plane while I was building it. I had about 300 hours flight time but not much taildragger experience. I had always thought I was a gutsy guy. After all, I had raced cars, hill-climbed with motorcycles, and so on; but I just couldn't bring myself to fly my new plane. I spent the next couple days taxing up and down the runway.

The Jersey Shore Airport is a grass runway between farm fields. A farmer, who had been working in his corn field while watching me taxi around, stopped his tractor and asked me why I didn't fly. When I told him the airplane was ready but I wasn't. He said, "Okay then, I'll fly it." Jersey Shore is only eight miles from Lock Haven, Pennsylvania where Piper Cubs were built from 1937 until the early 70s. And I think every farmer in the valley had owned one at one time or another. This farmer still had a 1946 J3 Cub. He slid into the left seat (I moved over to the right), fired it up, and taxied to the end of the runway. Without hesitation, he pushed the throttle full and pushed the stick forward until the tail came up and we took off!! We climbed to about 300 feet and flew around the pattern a couple of times. Then he said, "Got to land and get back to work." He landed the airplane, got out, and climbed back on his tractor and out through the field he went.

How Not to Make a First Flight in an RV-6
Doug Leihy

Early one morning while I was working on my new RV-6, my good friend Moore stopped by the hanger. He helped me tie up some loose ends and then suggested I do some high-speed taxi tests. He wanted me to lift the plane off the ground a couple of feet then land to be sure the plane would be stable and wouldn't roll.

I didn't want to do this. I would rather have continued installing the carpets or doing anything with the airplane other than lifting off the ground. Moore told me to go back and forth on runways 17 and 35 increasing the rpm's a little each time. He'd let me know when I was off the ground a foot or two with his handheld radio.

I had started to taxi uphill on runway 30 at 2,000 rpm when the plane jumped off the ground about halfway down the runway. Before I could do anything, I was about 30 feet in the air. I immediately cut power and lowered the nose, but then realized I was too high and going too fast to land safely. The only thing I could do at this point was give the plane full power and go around. I thought to myself, "How did I get here?" I never even did a mag check. I was petrified! Then on the radio I heard Moore say, "You're airborne." Duh! At 100 feet, I kind of knew I was airborne.

Moore's enthusiastic voice came back on the radio, and he suggested that he would take off in his plane to join me. "We could fly together, do airspeed checks, and try a few approach stalls; or maybe go to Oroville for your first landing."

My reply was a flat "No."

"What are your intentions?" Moore asked.

"To land" I said.

As I turned downwind, I noticed that I was breaking through 2,300 feet and climbing. I leveled the plane and noted the airspeed indicator was reading 180 mph. This was not good. I brought the rpm's down to 2,000 and was still going 170 mph. The engine that I installed on this aircraft had not been run in eight years.

I was very reluctant to pull back power, but I thought I had no choice. So I brought the power back to 900 rpm and held the nose up until the airspeed hit 100 mph. I turned base and put on 10 degrees of flap then turned final at 20 degrees of flap. Moore had to call my base and final because I was too scared to talk. This was probably the worst pattern ever flown at Paradise Airport, California.

When I landed on the main gear, I gave the stick a little backpressure. I apparently gave it a little up pressure instead because the push-to-talk wooden handle came off in my hand. This got my attention! I gave the plane full power, grabbed the stick again, and took off. The second time around the pattern was, thankfully, better than the first. I came around and landed to complete my first flight. After the first flight in my new RV-6 that I had built myself, my sense of pride was overwhelming. (So was that fact that I was still alive.)

A Pitts Story
Jeffrey Kaney

I'm an airplane guy—no, an airplane *nut*. Since I was a kid, I ate, drank, slept, and made it through 16 years of school daydreaming about airplanes. Big, slow, fast, or small I can see the beauty in almost all of them (except possibly the Navion). Anyway, now I'm entering my mid-thirties. My career is on track, and I have a wonderful, understanding wife. Now is the time for my daydream to become a reality. The next addition to our family will be an airplane. Not just any airplane my friend, no. Thou shall not covet, but *please* excuse this sin, for it is about a Curtis Pitts Special. Even saying those words gives me goose bumps. This won't be just an airplane; this will be a work of art. A vehicle that captures the imagination of ... well ... me! Yeah, me. You see, this is a single-seat beauty. Me! Me! Me! A purely selfish endeavor (remember—understanding wife).

For as long as I can remember, the one constant object of my desire—before cars, girls, and a good job—has been a red, white, and blue classic S1 Pitts. I can recall the airshows of the 1970s and 80s, when a little, red biplane would be trailing white smoke, making ribbons through the blue Midwestern sky. When I was a boy, those pilots were my Batman and the plane was my Batmobile.

After two years of reading every S1 ad in *Trade-A-Plane*, talking to anyone with Pitts knowledge, indoctrinating my seven-year-old boy (he thought they took "trick gas"), and dropping huge, not-to-subtle hints to my wife, the opportunity presented itself. There was a friend of a friend that had an amateur-built 1968 S1 with all of the options I was looking for. Best of all, the little plane was "tired."

This child needed new fabric, an engine overhaul, and an all-around rework. This made the price attractive.

My father has always said, "Don't push things too much. If it was meant to be it will happen." As much as I hate to admit it, he was right ... *again*. At the same time as this opportunity presented itself, I came across an ad offering fabric and engine work. I called Mike Williams in Columbus, Indiana. The next building block was in place. You see, I would *never* fly anything that I had built. Next and most importantly, my Super Woman said "Follow your dreams ... buy it." (Ain't she great!) Mike and his cohort, Barrett Brummett, were off the next week to inspect it; and in the matter of one week, I owned a ferry-capable Pitts Special.

Over the next ten months, Mike and I communicated almost daily via email on options, progress, and excitement. During this time, I took several hours of instruction from our friend Bruce Thalheimer in Naples, Florida. Bruce has a beautiful Pitts S2-C and is an outstanding instructor. I needed a nap after each lesson! I learned a lot of things; many I didn't even know I needed to know. Thanks to Bruce, my general flying is a lot safer.

I secured a hangar to give my new baby a home. Like an expectant parent, I bought all the accoutrements I could find. The nursery would be an uncluttered place. Tool sets, wash buckets, cloth flying helmet with goggles, lots of wax, degreasers and polishes, chocks, stepladder, flashlights, and a fridge.

On a cold windy day in April, I received the call I had been waiting for. My baby was about ready. After almost nine months, the day was almost here. I packed a few things and was off to help deliver my plane. I spent four days at Mike's fabulous shop finishing small items and getting to know him, 'er, the Pitts. Flown by Barrett, with Mike and I in the chase plane, our new baby arrived home on the 24th of April.

Rain—eight days of rain and wind followed. An airplane had never been so clean and a hanger so tidy. I was disappointed about the weather, but just the opportunity to be in the same room with the little guy was wonderful enough.

The big day finally came, sixty degrees, pure sun, and no wind. This was the day! On the way to the airport, I had to set the cruise control to keep from speeding. To say I was excited was an understatement. I now hoped and prayed that the airport would be quiet. I really didn't want an audience for my first flight.

As I pushed the little guy onto the tarmac, the sun shined off the fancy red paint and the stainless flying wires. After my preflight walk around, I realized that I couldn't remember anything I had just looked at. I was very excited and was rushing through everything. I took a walk around the hangers to calm down and to force myself to think straight. Things started to slow down. I accomplished a proper preflight and donned my new parachute with purpose.

After strapping the plane on, I fired him up and cautiously began my taxi. My wish was granted, and the airport was empty. At the end of the runway, run-up complete, I sat and ran through the S2-C takeoff in my mind. It was time to go. I taxied out and lined up, took in a few deep breaths—it was now or never. The throttle went forward and a deep roar bellowed ahead from the firewall. I dashed down the runway like a toddler about to be spanked. A little left, a little right, a little left, a little more left, Left, LEFT, little right, centered, nose forward, airborne at last! Climb, climb baby climb! Up we went, my hopefully soon-to-be friend and I climbed over the airport to about 4,000 feet. I think it was then that I finally took my first breath.

Things were happening so fast that I was in sensory overload. It took me back to my first flight in the T-38, except this time it was solo. How is the oil pressure? What should the oil temp be? Are all these sounds normal? With all those wings and wires, where is the level horizon picture? I decided to concentrate, one thing at a time, try to fly relativity straight and level. In my mind I talked to my friend, "OK boy, be good to me. No surprises and I'll keep you clean and well oiled. See, we are a team here, so work with me!"

I decided the best way to carry on a conversation with him was to explore the flight envelope. We did some stalls, slow flight, falling leaf maneuvers, and steep turns. All at once it hit me hard, why hadn't I considered this yet? I'm going to have to land this thing, and without a scratch. I listened hard to my new child. Hopefully he was not already the rebellious teenager. I started to think of all my friends and family that I had tried not to brag too much to. A ground loop would not be good. Great … the airport was quiet, but I felt as if everyone I knew was somehow watching me. Just the kind of pressure I didn't need.

It's now or never. Boy, I sure wish the grass runways were open. One low pass, slipping, looks good. Another low pass, slower, slipping looks … OK. Next one is going to be a touchdown. Crosswind, downwind, base final slipping, take a peek, too high, too fast, looks bad, go around again, next time for sure. Downwind, on speed and altitude; base, pitch and power—proper this time; sink—good, speed—OK, final, slip, peek, speed? Who has time to look! Touch down, roll out, stop, breathe, smile, relief!

On the taxi back, my smile turned to worry. Could I do this again? Was this a fluke? These thoughts will keep me awake tonight, I know it. So I did what I knew I had to do, taxied out for another takeoff.

Two more successful landings followed on that day. As I pulled my buddy back into the hangar, a sense a pride and accomplishment overwhelmed me. I accomplished a personal goal. Everything I have done in my life prepared me for this moment.

I wiped the bugs off the spinner and windscreen and closed the hangar door. Smiling, I took one last look at my Batmobile, hoping for another perfect Pitts flying day.

UFOs

Johnny Chakerian

I replaced the engines in my Stearman crop/spray aircraft to new 450 hp engines. I was to spray an oat field that day and my first load of spray was a full and heavy load.

I made my normal approach to the field, came over high power lines, and throttled back as I dropped down close to the field. I flared out and added power, but the engine backfired and I came down in the oats. They wrapped around the spray boom and wheels. The airplane was on the ground when the engine went to max power, which thankfully, kept the airplane from flipping over. The prop was now sucking up the oats and slinging them over the cockpit into my face. (Hurt like hell!) I couldn't do anything but keep the stick back and full power. All of a sudden, I was airborne with a bent and twisted spray boom.

A month later, the farmer came to pay his bill. He was telling me about a big hole in his oat field but didn't see tracks of any vehicles driving in and tearing out the oats. I told him people were reporting UFO sightings about that time. In an odd way you could say that I built and fly my first UFO.

AT THE EDGE OF THE ENVELOPE

There was a demon that lived in the air. They said whoever challenged him would die. His controls would freeze up, his plane would buffet wildly, and he would disintegrate. The demon lived at Mach 1 on the meter, seven hundred and fifty miles an hour, where the air could no longer move out of the way. He lived behind a barrier through which they said no man would ever pass. They called it the sound barrier.

-Ridley in the 1983 movie 'The Right Stuff'

First Flight in the X-15
Scott Crossfield

Jill wants a story, a first flight story. Now no self respecting fighter/ test pilot can turn down a request for a story. However in view of the hair raising tales she was raised on I have to stay out of that league and tell a fun first flight story, well mostly fun anyway.

The X-15 first flight was quite a day that took me nine years to get to. It was also an award winning record flight that day. On the X-15 first flight it was to be dropped from the B-52 at about 38,000 feet with no fuel on board, none, nada, so it was just a low L/D glider that gave the pilot precious little time to learn to fly.

On June 8, 1959 Captain Charlie Bock dropped me over Muroc Dry Lake after an agonizing number of captive flights all spring getting all the systems to work as advertised. Air launch is a beautiful way to get flying compared to the noisy commotion of a ground take off. I said a prayer, toggled the launch switch, and was a fledgling eaglet eager to spread my wings to begin the journey to the stars. The X-15 was an airplane, it flew like an airplane, a good airplane. It was a pleasant surprise.

I was determined to fly it with the side stick, my first, having been fighting to get rid of that ax handle between our legs since power controls came on the scene. The X-15 at those low speeds immediately proved to be an airplane with excellent aerodynamic harmony and control harmony. It was like kissing a beautiful virgin. I was very happy with what I found but really not surprised all that much. I did some increasing rate pitch, roll, and yaw maneuvers and some combinations at several speeds. I repeated with the flaps lowered. All were with pleasing response. The side stick was a natural with only wrist action needed for pitch and forearm roll for roll. It had no adverse yaw and the rudder response was like a bent wing Corsair.

Euphoric, I did a victory roll. The euphoria clouded judgment because I scooped out of that roll which was a warning that the elevators were not giving me what I asked for. I was quizzical for a moment but it was time to land this mother and turned my thought to the showdown. The second chapter rather got me up on the edge of my seat. First, Major Bob White, chasing, said the lower vertical fin didn't come off when I jettisoned it. Whoops, I now envisioned becoming the fastest plow in history as the fin stuck down below the rear landing skids. Bob then announced: "There it goes, how nice," I dropped the gear, lowered the flaps and was comfortable that everything was on the money.

Now, every pilot, upon occasion needs a good calibration of his conceit. Mine was due. I intended to land at 174 knots not 173 or 175. I flared to land at 174 and low and behold this creature had a mind of its own and began to appear to have a severe classic static instability and diverged in pitch with each control input. That, by its nature, created a pilot induced oscillation that I didn't think was good promise for longevity that close to the ground. The old pro had only one mission in life in those moments: to land at the bottom of an oscillation or become a very expensive ball of scrap metal, without warranty, tearing up the lake bed and spoiling Becky's Father's Day.

Of course a heavy sigh was appropriate when I did land sans structural damage. Bob White said, "Very nice!" I answered, "What did you expect from the old pro?" But, the conceit calibration was not yet complete. The long flare put me into an unintended area on the lake bed and the X-15 was heading for an erosion ditch still at a pretty good clip. My kindergarten class was not over and I learned more. Instinctively I put in hard left rudder and full left roll control. The rolling tail loaded the left skid and the airplane turned left. The rudder countered that roll to a degree but putting in right rudder added to the load on the left skid and I quickly found that one could significantly turn the X-15 on "roll" out. It was a very educational day.

Stormy loved the barrel roll but blasphemed my ancestry for my conclusion that the airplane was statically unstable in pitch on landing. It turns out he was right and it was a control system problem. All in all it was a very educational day leading to significant celebration.

Oh! The record and award? The Southern California Soaring Society awarded me a unique trophy of a red brick milled into a tear drop shape beautifully mounted on a similar shape piece of mahogany with an engraved brass plaque declaring me the holder of the world's record for the shortest time from 38,000 feet to the ground as a glider, 3 minutes and 58 seconds. The X-15 broke that record on the third powered flight.

Jill that is my yarn, Scott.

Yeager's X-1A Flight
Daphne Myrann

On December 12, 1953, Chuck Yeager, after returning from an early morning bird hunt, stepped out of his Model A Ford and walked toward us. "Mornin'," he drawled in his West Virginian accent. His face broke into a smile, and his blue eyes crinkled as he got into the station wagon with Sil Sartore and me.

Sil, my boss, and I delivered Chuck to the Bell hangar where two men helped him into his partial pressure suit. Then we took him to the B-29 for Flight No. 10. The B-29 was ready with the X-1A in its belly, and it was piloted by Harold Russell with Danny Grubaugh, as the co-pilot. Bell personnel were already onboard. The two F-86 chase planes, flown by Jack Ridley and Kit Murray, were airborne and waiting for the B-29 to take off.

When the B-29 was airborne, the chase planes' duties were to fly alongside and under the B-29 to observe the condition of both ships. The chase planes had to circle continually because of the prop wash and their difficulty maintaining the slower speed.

Immediately after the B-29 had taxied to the lakebed, a caravan of Bell Aircraft and Air Force personnel, fire trucks, and ambulance vehicles all with their bright orange and white checkered flags, made their way to a spot near the projected landing area. It was early morning, crisp and clear, with a violet-blue sky. One of the vehicles was equipped with a loudspeaker, which enabled personnel on the lakebed to hear the conversations between airplanes and ground control. There were 27 people: rocket engineers, Air Force pilots, rocket technicians, specialized mechanics, my boss, and me. Bell also permitted the business office staff to attend. My job was to record by shorthand all conversation that transpired during the flight. Fortunately, it was also recorded on tape.

When the B-29 reached 8,000 feet, Chuck entered the X-1A. He had to check the panel instruments, check his oxygen on the pressure suit he was wearing, and make sure his canopy was down and locked. Chuck had a green flight-plan card on a metal container that fit on his knee. Actually, I had first typed the flight plan on a white card, but at high altitude, it was discovered that the brilliance of the sunlight on the white card made it unreadable. Hence, the green card.

After confirming that all was secure at 32,000 feet, Chuck informed the B-29 that he was ready to be released from its belly. The chase planes were beside him when Harold, the B-29 pilot, started the countdown: "Five, four, three, two, one." Then Dan (the copilot) said, "DROP!" and released the X-1A. Chuck went into a graceful glide that carried him ahead of the lumbering B-29.

There are four rocket cylinders on the X-1A; each of which has to be lit for forward power. Each cylinder delivers 1,500 pounds of thrust. Chuck successfully lit them one at a time. With three of the cylinders lit, he was climbing rapidly. When he lit the fourth cylinder, he was at 70,000 feet and out of everyone's sight, including the chase planes.

The F-86s were restricted to 40,000 feet altitude at that time. Upon lighting that fourth cylinder, the power thrust Chuck back into his seat. He went to 73,000 feet. His words, "At 73,000 feet. Here goes. Push over!" could be heard on the radio. As he pushed the stick forward to go over the top of the arc, his Mach meter read 2.5 Mach (2 1/2 times the speed of sound), which was faster than any human had gone before.

On the ground, we could not see Chuck after the bomber dropped him from its belly. We shaded our eyes and looked in vain. We listened. The loudspeakers were on, and we held our breath. Everyone knew this was a very dangerous flight for Chuck.

A deathly silence interrupted by static was all we could hear. No one in the chase planes or the B-29 spoke. Everyone feared there was trouble. We waited and waited to hear from Chuck. Later, we learned that when the X-1A went over the arc, it went completely out of control. The controls had nothing to grab onto in the rarefied air of high altitude. It was like a feather being blown by the wind. Chuck was subjected to negative, positive, and zero-G's. (One "G" is equal to his weight, and he pulled eight G's or eight times his weight.) His pressure suit protected him, but his body tossing about the cockpit was horrendous. He even cracked the inner canopy with his helmet.

After an interminable amount of time, he finally came down to 25,000 feet and into heavier air, which enabled the X-1A to stabilize. He had fallen 50,000 feet (almost 10 miles). Meanwhile, no one on the ground or in the air knew what had transpired. We all anxiously waited and feared the worst. Could Chuck be lost? What happened to him? We waited, but the silence persisted.

Finally, Chuck radioed in, but as he came on the air, he gave a loud gasp and said, "I'm at 25,000." "I don't know where I am. I'm hurt—I think I'm over the Tehachapi Mountains."

Ridley and Murray in the chase planes could not find him. They were desperately searching, as was the B-29, which had turned on its axis in order to look in every direction. This maneuver threw people in the rear askew, but they knew Chuck had to be found quickly.

The effect on all of us on the lakebed was profound. Hearing Chuck gasping and knowing he was injured was shocking. One of the engineers lost his stomach, a rocket engineer dropped to his knees in prayer, and other men had tears running down their faces. My shorthand grew from the usual one-half inch to two inches, then stopped.

Silence prevailed again for another ten seconds—each second like a lifetime. We all knew his ship had no power and was coming down at an alarming rate. Due to the lakebed's vastness and flatness, depth perception makes it extremely difficult for a pilot to land as there are no reference points—it's like landing in the middle of the ocean. The chase plane had to fly alongside the X-1A on landing and advise Chuck as to how many feet there were from his plane to the lakebed.

Murray did not reach Chuck until the X-1A was over the runway. Murray confirmed the airplane's gear and flaps were down. He said, "Coming off fifty now, Chuck" (meaning fifty feet over the lakebed)

"Now twenty—twenty yet, Chuck … five … two … one … looks good, Chuck, looks fine!"

When they came in, Chuck's plane and the chase ship were only 10 feet off the ground as they flew in front of us. When they landed, it was a moment that united all of us.

Immediately, Sil and I ran to the station wagon and drove to Chuck. Two mechanics in a jeep followed us; they had to crawl on the fuselage of the X-1A to remove clamps that held the canopy so that Chuck could get out.

Chuck once again sat beside me while Sil drove. He wasted no time, "What a ride. My back hurts." Neither Sil nor I had much to say. We were so thankful that he was there. It was quite a contrast to several hours earlier when we delivered him to the airplane. Incidentally, the airplane did not suffer any damage except for the inner canopy that Chuck broke with his helmet.

One of the mechanics, Bonjie, who was artistic, removed the inner canopy and made cutouts of the X-1A complete with a band of frost etched on it. He mounted the cutouts on bronze. This bronze was etched with the date, airplane, speed, and our names. The bronze was mounted on velvet, which was tightly drawn on an 8-by-10-inch piece of wood and framed. Bonjie gave one of these priceless souvenirs to each Bell person involved and one to Chuck, of course. My treasure is in a very protected place.

Being a part of historical moments like these create memories that are never forgotten. I can still taste the fear and feel the relief of having Chuck safely sitting next to me. What a ride indeed!

Piggy Backing the Shuttle
Fitzhugh L. Fulton Jr.

I am not sure that this should be called a "first flight" because the Boeing 747 was a well-proven airplane by the time of this test program. However, the shuttle had never been airborne, and of course, the combined 747 and shuttle had not yet been flown. The mated vehicles were an impressive sight and were jokingly referred to as the "world's largest biplane." The 747 was officially titled the "Shuttle Carrier Aircraft" or SCA.

The selection of the Boeing 747 as the carrier airplane was a long and careful process. Several proposals for a carrier airplane were studied. One proposal even had two 747 fuselages, with the shuttle carried between the fuselages. Another was a completely new airplane with a very long, straight wing. Yet, the wingspan and width of the landing gear was so large, it could have operated from only a few airfields. The final selection was between an Air Force Lockheed C-5 transport and a commercial Boeing 747. Either airplane could have the shuttle mounted on top, and they were equally acceptable. An attempt to get a C-5 from the Air Force was turned down. (Obtaining one would have been a big money-saver for NASA's shuttle program.) However, the Air Force needed all of its C-5s for military airlift requirements, so the 747 became the shuttle carrier of choice.

At that time period, there was an excess of Boeing 747 airplanes. Several airlines had surplus airplanes in a "flyable storage" status. American Airlines was one of the airlines with 747s that were not being used. NASA arranged to purchase one of their airplanes for approximately $15.8 million. That was a bargain! Since NASA was getting an American Airlines airplane, it was logical to get our training with American. Pilots and flight engineers went to American's flight academy in Fort Worth, Texas, and completed the ground school and simulator courses that all airline pilots complete. Then we did a few flights in our 747 with American Airline instructor pilots. That was followed by an FAA checkride to become type-rated in the 747. The flight crews that were checked out at that time were Tom McMurtry and I as the pilots, and Victor Horton and Louis (Skip) Guidry as the flight engineers. All of us were from the NASA Dryden Flight Research Center at Edwards Air Force Base except for Guidry, who was from the Johnson Space Center in Houston. I was designated as the Primary Project Pilot.

About that time, a "wake vortex" program was funded and scheduled. The NASA 747 was to be the airplane to generate the wake vortex. That gave the NASA flight crewmembers an excellent opportunity to become more proficient in the airplane. A set of smoke generators was installed on the wing of the 747. A variety of airplanes were then flown behind the 747 in the wake that was generated and visually displayed by the smoke. Upon completion of the wake vortex program, the airplane was flown to Seattle for modifications by the Boeing Company.

The contract with Boeing called for them to modify the airplane to carry the shuttle and to do a short series of flight tests afterward to check for flutter and acceptability of the modifications. In the meantime, there were many engineering studies that were carried out by NASA, the Air Force, the Boeing Company, Rockwell (the shuttle manufacturer), and other companies. The flight crews flew simulations of the 747 carrying the shuttle. We also made many simulated launches of the shuttle. Some were in Seattle at Boeing; others were in Dallas at the LTV Company where there were dual simulators. The 747 pilot could fly one simulator through a launch while one of the astronauts could fly the other simulator down to a landing.

The 747 modifications included installing dual, fixed 20- by 10-foot vertical stabilizers and also forward and aft struts to support the shuttle. Most passenger convenience items and all but a few of the passenger seats were removed. There were also some modifications made to the hydraulic and electrical systems. A Boeing crew, headed by my friend, Paul Bennett, made the first few flights on the airplane to clear the flutter envelope. After that, I flew with Bennett on most of the Boeing test flights. On one of the last Boeing flights, the plan was to fly down to Edwards Air Force Base in California and work with the NASA control room to make sure the airplane and the NASA control room were compatible. Paul said he would make the takeoff and fly down to Edwards, and I would then take the airplane and work with the control room. When complete, I would fly back to Seattle and make the landing.

Paul had been a heavy smoker for years but was making a big effort to quit. He was cutting down a little at a time and was using special gum to help him. The day we took off to go to Edwards was the first day that Paul was to go completely off cigarettes. He was quite excited about getting to the point where he would be off cigarettes. We had just gotten off the ground when he announced, "that was the first takeoff that I've made since I quit smoking." His exuberance diminished as the flight went on, and then he became very quiet. I could tell that he was suffering, but to his credit, he quit smoking that day and stayed a non-smoker.

Once the testing at Boeing was complete, and we had ferried the airplane to Edwards, there was much to do. More instrumentation was installed, and an escape system was designed and installed in the airplane. Without special modifications, there was no way to exit the 747 airplane during flight, and there was some concern that the shuttle might contact the 747 after being released, making an emergency egress by the crew necessary. A decision was made to install a "laundry chute" type of emergency escape system. This exit was located 20 feet behind the cockpit, and when the pilot actuated a special switch, a hole would be explosively cut through the fuselage and out the bottom of the airplane. The crew members, who were already wearing parachutes and special helmets that would protect their eyes and provide needed oxygen in case any dangerous gases were presents, would make their way to the escape chute by using guide ropes that were located on the floor. We all hoped that we would never have to use this escape system, but it was comforting to know that it was there.

The shuttle Enterprise arrived at the NASA facility on January 31, 1977, after being towed 36 miles through the city of Lancaster and across the Edwards Air Force Base test area. The Enterprise was the only shuttle that would never go into space. It was primarily air launched and then flown to a landing to allow astronauts to get some flight experience before they went into space, and also to determine the reliability of the craft's operating systems. It was given a thorough check and prepared for flight by NASA and Rockwell employees. Many hours of engineering and operational meetings were held before all the desired tests were incorporated into the flight plans.

Finally the Enterprise was ready and was loaded on top of the 747. The test plan was complete, the support personnel were fully trained, management had given their approval, and the flight crew was more than ready. On February 15, 1977, we boarded the 747 for a series of taxi tests. The gross weight of the combined vehicles was approximately 585,000 pounds, which was much less than the maximum allowable weight of 710,000 pounds. I was in the left seat, and Tom McMurtry was in the right seat. Vic Horton and Skip Guidry shared the flight engineer duties. We always flew with two flight engineers so that one could be at the panel and the other could check things in the back of the airplane if necessary. Three taxi runs were made with the fastest one at about 135 knots. Everything went well. We confirmed that the nose wheel would come completely off the ground if we set takeoff power immediately after brake release. Although this is the normal procedure on a commercial airliner, it is not acceptable on the shuttle carrier aircraft because of the high vertical center of gravity. The preferred procedure was to gradually increase engine thrust after the brakes were released while holding full down elevator. Full power could be set by the time the speed had reached 60 knots, and the elevator control could be relaxed to near neutral at the same time. We also found that when nearing takeoff speed the elevator was fully effective. We lifted the nose wheel and put it down with excellent control response. All other systems checked out fine. The flight crew felt that the mated airplane was ready to fly.

Three days later, on February 18, the first flight was flown at a takeoff gross weight of 583,500 pounds. The same flight crew was aboard. One of the things that we always had to have on board during each flight was the key to the shuttle launch system and the key to the escape system. Both systems used pyrotechnics for activation, so the keys were kept in the safe in my office. (On one later occasion, I forgot about the keys until I reached the airplane and had to send back for them.) On this day we had everything and were on the airplane and ready to go earlier than scheduled. Our ground crew and the other support personnel always did an outstanding job of getting the 747 and the shuttle ready to go.

We started engines and taxied out with support vehicles, ambulances, and fire trucks following us. Skip was at the flight engineer's panel, and Vic was making power calculations and reviewing the takeoff data for us. There was some mild vertical bumping as we taxied out at speeds of 10 to 20 knots. It was of no concern but had not been noted during the taxi runs. The T-38 chase and photo airplanes took off, and we taxied onto the runway for takeoff. After an OK from our control room and from the tower, we released brakes and started accelerating. Tom called off the speeds as we accelerated. At 142 knots, I pulled back on the control column to rotate up to a pitch attitude of seven degrees. A pitch attitude of 13 degrees would be normal for a standard airline 747. At 13 degrees on this airplane, the vertical stabilizers on the tip of the horizontal stabilizers would have scraped the runway. We lifted off at 153 knots after a ground roll of about 6,000 feet. The chase airplanes joined up and gave us an OK on the outside visual check. We noted that there was continuous light airframe buffet. The maximum altitude and speed during the flight were 16,000 feet and 250 knots respectively. The handling characteristics were good throughout the speed range in which we flew. We completed a series of airspeed calibration points with an Air Force T-37 pacer airplane, and then we cleared the flutter envelope through coordination with the control room. Elevator, aileron, and rudder raps were done to check stability. Response was good in all cases. The airplane was quite sensitive directionally and seemed to be quite happy to fly just slightly out of trim. It was no problem, but any minor difference in thrust between the number one and number four engines resulted in a very small side-slip angle.

I had requested that we do a simulated approach to a landing at altitude. That was done, and it showed that the engine power needed for final approach was close to that needed in the simulator. The only other test that I had requested to be included in the flight plan was a look at minimum control speed. The airplane was flown down to 122 knots with the number four engine at idle power while the other engines were set at maximum continuous power. There was sufficient rudder control to handle the thrust asymmetry. That showed that the minimum control speed characteristics were good. During the flight, Vic had made one trip back into the cabin area to check things. He found that there was no abnormal buffeting on the shuttle or on the 747 surfaces. However, he did find strong high frequency noise in the area below the shuttle attach points that was later measured to be in the 130 to 135 decibel range.

We made a straight-in approach to the runway. The landing was not much different than in a standard 747. There was a slight nose down trim change as the power was reduced to idle. Only reverse thrust was needed to slow to taxi speed. Slight braking was used when turning off the runway. It had been a great flight, and we felt that the test program could continue as planned.

There were four more mated flights with the shuttle unmanned. These were to obtain additional engineering data and to gather data for the operational handbook. After that, three flights were flown with the shuttle manned. There were two crews. Fred Haise and Gordon Fullerton were on one crew, and Joe Engle and Dick Truly were on the other crew. These manned flights were primarily designed to run tests on the space shuttle and for the astronauts to learn how the systems operated. The 747 shuttle carrier aircraft was only used to take the shuttle to the desired flight condition. The crews were also preparing for the launches from on top of the 747. We observed that any time the astronauts opened the speed brakes or moved the flight controls, we could feel it in the 747. The shuttle speed brakes were very effective. Full open required a large power increase to maintain speed. Several flight tracks were flown in the 747 that were similar to the track planned for the actual launches.

Next came the five launches from on top of the 747. The astronauts took turns making the launch flights with Haise and Fullerton taking the first turn. All of the launches and the landings went as planned. The shuttle had a large tail cone installed for all mated flights except the last two launch flights. The tail cone made the airflow around the rear of the shuttle smoother and it also reduced buffet on the shuttle carrier airplane. On the launches where the tail cone was installed, the shuttle carrier airplane was flown to approximately 28,000 feet where a slight dive was established. When reaching 276 knots indicated airspeed at about 25,000 feet, the throttles were reduced to idle power and the speed brakes extended. It took a few seconds to restabilize, and then we called out "launch ready." The shuttle pilot immediately hit the launch switch, and the two aircraft separated cleanly. The 747 turned left, and the shuttle turned right. The T-38 chase and photo airplanes confirmed that everything was satisfactory. The shuttle will always return from space with the tail cone removed. In that configuration, the 747 experienced continuous moderate airframe buffet. The last two launches were done with the tail cone removed. They were similar to the earlier launches except that the 747 could not climb as high due to the extra buffet and drag. The launch altitude was 22,000 feet, and the launch speed was less. No problems were encountered.

The final test phase was in the ferry configuration. That meant that the front strut between the 747 and the shuttle was shortened to bring the nose of the shuttle down. That reduced drag and provided better performance during ferry operations. The angle of incidence was previously set at six degrees but was now lowered to three degrees. There was very little difference noticeable in the cockpit, but the fuel usage during cruise was less. While carrying the shuttle after a maximum gross weight takeoff of 710,000 pounds, the fuel use was still very high. The initial cruise altitude was only 13,000 to 14,000 feet, and total fuel flow was approximately 40,000 pounds per hour. A commercial airline 747 cruising at a higher altitude needs only about 20,000 pounds of fuel per hour. The mated shuttle carrier airplane is limited to a speed of 250 knots indicated speed or a Mach number of six-tenths the speed of sound. That results in a cruising speed that is only about two-thirds the speed of an airliner.

Since the initial testing, the 747 has been used to ferry all of the shuttles, whenever and wherever they are needed. One of the most significant ferry flights was on July 4, 1982. President Reagan was at Edwards Air Force Base to see the landing of the shuttle Columbia which was returning from a mission in space. After Columbia's landing, I made a takeoff in the 747 carrying the shuttle Challenger on the way to Florida. President Reagan gave us our takeoff clearance on the radio. We then flew by the crowd and the presidential review party at about 400 feet. Two young observers sitting on the ramp that day to watch the shuttle landing and the flyby were my 12-year-old grandson, Jason, and the author of this book, Jill Rutan Hoffman. That was over 25 years ago.

Chasing the Space Shuttle
Jim C. Ross

This story begins many years ago ... 1992 to be exact. I had just started my flight career as an aerial photographer at NASA's Dryden Flight Research Center located at Edwards Air Force Base, California. I had been a ground support photographer at Dryden for two years prior to this, and I already had extensive experience with space shuttle operations on the ground. However, it was my dream to expand my horizons and actually fly in a chase plane alongside a space shuttle. I knew I would never be approved to photo chase an actual orbiter landing, and therefore, I felt my best chance would be on a ferry flight.

In the fall of 1992, I approached Dryden's Director for Flight Operations, Tom McMurtry, who also happened to be a shuttle carrier aircraft pilot, and asked him about the possibilities of providing photo chase of an orbiter ferry flight to update our file photos. He said that although it was a very difficult and involved process he would look into it for me. He called later to informed me that he had made some inquiries, and unfortunately, the individuals in charge of ferry flights at the Johnson Space Center were not in favor of my request unless there was a real "hard" requirement. I thanked Tom and with much regret, decided that it was just not meant to be.

From 1996 to the fall of 2000, the orbiter landings took place at NASA's Kennedy Space Center in Florida. They were, however, still flown via the shuttle carrier aircraft from Florida to Plant 42 in Palmdale, California, to be refurbished (a process that took approximately one year) and then returned to Kennedy. During this time, I sat in California and waited. Finally, after four and a half

years, the Space Shuttle Discovery made its way back to Edwards
… but, I'm getting a little ahead of myself.

During this time, Dryden acquired a new pilot from NASA's
Johnson Space Center named Mark "Forger" Stucky. Mark
approached me one day and asked if I had ever chased an orbiter
ferry flight. (My dream!) I replied that I had once looked into the
possibility but was not given permission. Mark said that since he
had just come from Johnson and knew the right people to call, that
if I was still interested he could arrange it. Boy—Oh Boy!! Was I
interested!?! You bet!!! A few days later, Mark called to say that
he had arranged the flight and that Dryden and Johnson Flight
Operations were "cool" with it. In closing, he said that he would be
"in touch." My prayers were answered!

Space Shuttle Atlantis was being refurbished at this time at Plant
42. It was late in the summer of 1998, and Atlantis was going to be
ready for transport in the early fall. I was extremely excited that
everything was coming together so easily.

As September approached, I was unfortunately faced with a major
dilemma. My NASA technical monitor, Lee Duke, came to Lori
Losey, Dryden's Television Work Group Lead, and me to propose a
trip for the two of us to Moscow, Russia, to cover Dryden test pilot
Gordon Fullerton's pilot evaluation flights of the TU-144LL.

What is the old saying—"When it rains, it pours?" Well, it
was coming down by the bucketful! I had always wanted to go to
Moscow, and I was now faced with having to choose between two of
my "dreams." I weighed both options and decided to go to Russia.

At the same time, ironically, Mark Stucky had had a change of
plans and was not able to fly the space shuttle chase mission either.
To make a long story short, the mission was still a "go" when Dana
Purifoy, a Dryden test pilot, stepped in for Mark, and Carla Thomas,
a Dryden photographer, took my place in the backseat. They flew
during a beautiful, early morning sunrise, and Carla took some truly
stunning photo images of the ferry flight.

In 2000, following the landing of Space Shuttle Discovery, I
proposed that we shoot more in-flight space shuttle ferry photos.
Some of the pictures that Carla had shot were a little dim due to
the sun's position. I was hoping that by doing another ferry-flight

chase, we would be able to get some brighter images. I ran it though the appropriate channels once again and this time, it was approved. I was finally going to fly with the shuttle! My friend, pilot Mark Stucky, had recently taken a job with United Airlines, and had left Dryden. Dick Ewers, a Dryden test pilot, was to be the pilot for my mission. We made arrangements to chase the Shuttle Discovery on its way back to Florida after it had been repaired at Dryden's California Facility.

If you haven't noticed yet, there is a theme to this story thus far—disappointment and missed opportunities. I was determined that I *would not miss* this chance. The turn around team ran into some problems planning the return trip for Discovery, and the departure date slipped a few days right into an X-38 crew recovery vehicle mission. In order to support the X-38 missions, all pilots, photographers, and aircraft are needed. Dick and I were pulled off yet another chance at the obiter and assigned to chase the X-38 instead. We were able to see the ferry flight about 20,000 feet below us, not an optimal distance for photographs, but we were in the air at the same time, which was one step closer to my dream.

A few months later, in February, Space Shuttle Columbia was wrapping up its refurbishing at Plant 42. Fred Johnsen, NASA Dryden's News Chief, called to ask me if we could provide ground photo coverage of the ferry flight preparations of Columbia for a news release for the 20th anniversary of Space Shuttle Columbia's first flight. I saw my opportunity and grabbed it with both hands. I said that we could and asked him if he would be interested in getting some in-flight photos as well to support the press release. Fred got the "thumbs-up" from NASA Dryden and Johnson management. Meanwhile, I talked with Dryden pilot Gordon Fullerton, who was one of the shuttle carrier aircraft pilots, and asked about the feasibility. He said that he thought we would have a two-seat F-18 available, and since he was not involved in the ferry flight operation, he would fly with me. Everything appeared to be coming together. But, hey—I had been down this path before.

The weather for the flight path all across the country must be considered when ferrying the shuttle from California to Florida or vice versa. For safety reasons, the orbiter cannot be flown through inclement weather. As we got closer to the proposed flight day, the weather became downright fickle. It rained—*Oh Boy, did it rain*!! And not just in Palmdale. When the sky was clear in the Midwest, it would be raining in California. When it was raining in the Midwest it would be clear in the South ... well, you get the picture. So we waited—day after day ... after day.

Then another obstacle reared its ugly head. The runway at Edwards was scheduled to be closed the same weekend as our chase. The shuttle carrier pilots, Ace Beall and Frank Marlow, from NASA's Johnson Space Center, told us the mission was still on if the weather cleared up over the weekend. I thought for sure we were done. Fortunately, Gordon had made arrangements with Plant 42 to allow us to ferry our F-18 to their facility so that we could still complete our chase over the weekend. I was still in there, or so I thought.

The weekend came and went ... and more rain. Following a weather brief that stated that there was no possibility for a flight on Monday, Gordon and I brought the F-18 back to Dryden. At about the same time, the crew of Atlantis had been forced to land at Edwards due to bad weather at Cape Canaveral. And if the weather was not enough of a headache, Atlantis was getting ready to be flown out on the same day as Columbia. "Goodbye photo chase," I thought.

A decision had to be made as to which orbiter was going to go first. Then someone asked if we had enough people to crew both of the shuttle carrier aircraft so that they could fly the same day. It was finally decided that there were enough people, and therefore, both Columbia and Atlantis were scheduled to fly on March 1, 2001. Because of the dual-flight operation, Gordon had been reassigned to ferry Atlantis, leaving me without a pilot. Once again, I thought I was out of luck. Fortunately, the decision was made that the photo chase would go as scheduled. And once again, Dick Ewers was selected to be my pilot. The mission, however, was far from being a "sure thing."

Finally, it was the morning of the chase. It was like my birthday and Christmas all rolled into one, and I was ready to get started. I raced into the pilot's office only to find that the flight had been delayed and that we should stand by. I went back to my office and began to pace. About an hour later, I got the call—the flight was on! Our new takeoff time put us about one and one-half hours ahead of Atlantis.

Dick and I suited up and headed out to our jet. Our take-off went without a hitch. We were finally headed to Palmdale. Our arrival time would put us in approximately fifteen minutes prior to Columbia's departure. When we arrived at Palmdale everything looked good except for one thing—The Air Force KC-135 that was being used as the pathfinder aircraft had yet to take off, and it should have departed just prior to our arrival. The maintenance staff was fixing an instrumentation problem with the KC-135, and once it was fixed, the pathfinder and Columbia could take off.

Meanwhile, we had been in an airborne pattern for approximately 45 minutes over the hundreds of people who had gathered to see Columbia depart, when I heard what I had been waiting 10 years to hear: "The Columbia flight is go for takeoff." The KC-135, now fixed, took off without any further problems, and the ferry aircraft with Columbia began its long taxi to the runway. We did a few more orbits with our circles becoming tighter and tighter and the G's becoming higher and higher as Dick tried to time his airborne pick-up just right. As always, Dick was "spot on" with his spacing, and we paralleled the orbiter down the runway.

I began the flight by shooting video and shot continuously until the orbiter had turned out over Palmdale. As we continued east, I swapped between photo and video like a crazed madman. The day was perfect, and I could not get enough. The sun was shining and there were many fluffy clouds in the area, something we don't get very often in the high desert. Dick was the perfect pilot; he positioned our plane exactly where I needed to be to take great pictures. We were a prefect team.

Because of the delay, we only had enough fuel to stay with the orbiter for approximately 30 minutes. When we reached Twenty-Nine Palms, Dick told me I was going to have to "wrap it up" because we were "bingo fuel." At that point, he asked me if I would like to do a maneuver over the top of Columbia and possibly get a shot looking straight down on the two airplanes. I said, "Absolutely!"

I shot photos on the first over-the-top and then asked if we could go back over so that I could shoot one in video. He agreed, so I grabbed the video camera. But in moving the camera around the cockpit so much, it had become stuck in a setting that I could not figure out how to change. Since I am only a back-up videographer, I didn't have the expertise to do a quick fix. Dick kept telling me to let him know when I was ready, and I kept stalling. Finally, I put the video camera down and shot again on regular film. As it tuned out, it was lucky for me that the video camera died, since an image that I shot on the second over-the-top was selected as the winning photo of Aviation Week and Space Technology's 2001 Photo Contest.

While heading back, Dick called base operations and asked about the Atlantis. Our aircraft scheduler, Judy Duffield, told us that it had just taken off. Dick figured we would probably be able to intercept it over Boron, California, just east of Edwards. Since we were low on fuel, we shot just a few images of Atlantis before moving on.

Just when we reached the eastern shore of Rogers Dry Lakebed, we heard that NASA's ER-2 aircraft was coming down in altitude and would be landing shortly at Edwards. Dick checked the fuel, said we had a bit left, and asked me if I wanted to get some images of the ER-2. He called the ER-2 pilot and asked his permission to take a few pictures. The pilot approved it, and after we found him, we shot some photos of the ER-2 in descent. After a few minutes, we were at "joker fuel" and directly over the base. Dick called the tower and arranged for a straight-in approach, which was granted.

Just as we were about to land, I recall Dick saying that the taxpayers really got their money's worth out of that flight. I would definitely have to agree with him! What a day!!

First Flights at Scaled Composites
Mike Melvill

The flights that mean more to a test pilot than all others, the "gold star" flights, are the "first flights." That is to say, the first time a brand-new design lifts off the ground and goes flying. The second flight of such an airplane is not as prestigious to a test pilot, nor are first flights in follow-on aircraft, or the subsequent production aircraft after the original prototype.

I have been extremely fortunate in my career, and I have flown the first flights of eight of Burt's amazing new designs. These include N80RA, his model 72 Grizzly, a canard bush plane. Next was a self-launching sailplane, N81RA, his model 77 Solitaire. Then came N480AG, his model 120 Predator, a high-aspect-ratio crop duster. This was followed by N935SC, his model 144, the CM44, a first attempt at a somewhat stealthy and ultimately unmanned aircraft. Next came N187RA, the model 81 Catbird, a five-place, single-engine, high-speed transportation machine. This was followed by N62270, his model 226 Quiver D1. Then came N24BT, Burt's model 202 Boomerang, an asymmetrical, turbo-charged, high-performance, light twin that he designed and built for his own personal use. This was followed by the model 281 Proteus, N281PR, a one-of-a-kind, twin-engine jet designed to carry large external payloads to altitudes above 60,000 feet.

Most aircraft companies spend years testing their new designs in the form of models in wind tunnels and analyzing the results. We do not use wind tunnels. We prefer to test our designs in the real wind tunnel, up in the sky! This doesn't mean that we don't do all we can to try to understand how it may fly, what its handling qualities will be like, etc. There is always the element of risk that it may not perform as intended, and that is what makes this job so challenging and so exciting. It does however, require a lot of faith in our chief designer and the engineers who work under him.

There is no thrill to match the feeling of sitting in the cockpit of a brand-new, un-flown airplane, holding the brakes, and bringing the engine up to full power. What will the next few seconds bring? I know that I feel several emotions at such a time: I am a little apprehensive, I have a nervous feeling in my stomach, and I have an overwhelming desire not to overlook anything. As soon as I release the brakes and she starts to move forward, all of these feelings go away; now it is just the plane and me. How does she steer? How about acceleration? Can I feel the stick coming to life as the speed builds? Yes! The elevators are alive, so are the ailerons and rudders. As we approach lift-off speed, I take note of the position of the stick and rudders. Are they close to centered? This indicates a straight airplane. If I should find the stick in one corner, I would abort. As we become airborne, just a few inches from the ground, I carefully check the controls for proper direction and effectiveness. Then we are away from the runway environment, the chase plane is onboard, and this becomes a pretty normal test flight.

I won't bore you with detailed descriptions of each of these first flights. To be honest, in most cases they were routine, almost boring events just as we fervently hoped that they would be. However, there were inevitably a few memorable moments!

Boomerang Hits the Dirt

The first flight of the Boomerang was one of those memorable moments. Right after takeoff, the oil temperature on the left engine began to rise at more than a normal rate. I reduced power on the left engine, but the trend continued. Rather than ruin a new engine, I returned to the airport and prepared to land. I had maximum power on the right engine and just above idle on the left. There were no handling problems at all as I lowered the landing gear and noted three green lights. Our chase plane, a Beech Duchess, was in position at my 4 o'clock and confirmed that the gear appeared to be down.

Having already done several high-speed taxi and runway liftoffs, I had a good feel for the speed to fly and the sight picture in the landing flare. I made a normal landing on runway 12 at Mojave. As she slowed during the landing roll-out, the left wing began to drop. My first thought was that the left main strut had gone flat, but as was confirmed later from the chase video, the left main gear had actually retracted! I used all of the available right aileron, but inevitably, the left wing tip settled to the runway and began to drag the Boomerang to the left side of the runway. I applied the right brake in an attempt to keep her on the runway, but this brake soon overheated and quit working. At this point, I realized we were going to depart the left side of the runway. I pulled both mixture controls to idle cut-off and shut off both fuel valves.

The Boomerang left the runway and started across the dirt directly toward a concrete abutment and a small earth berm. She was slowing all the time, but not enough. The nose gear and right main both struck the concrete block and folded back; both props, still turning, struck the ground and wrapped around the spinners. We struck the earth berm, and she buried her nose in the dirt and pitched her tail into the air. For a second, I thought she would go over on her back, but fortunately, she fell back onto her belly, upright and level.

I looked out of the windshield and saw a fireman clad in a silver suit holding a fire hose. I was amazed that he had arrived so soon, but the fire crew had been standing by when they saw the left main collapse. They drove to where they predicted we would end up, and they were right there on the scene! The right brake had gotten so hot that it set fire to the right tire, and the fireman instantly extinguished the small fire.

There was considerable damage to the nose and right main gear, some minor scrape damage to the left wing tip and both lower cowlings, and both props were completely destroyed. There was no structural damage to the airframe. The left main had collapsed due to an incorrectly adjusted drag link on the left main gear. With the help of an enthusiastic Scaled crew, Burt was able to repair all of the damage, and we were flying again just three weeks after this incident!

Quiver's Adverse Yaw Saves the Day

Most of the time, at least in my experience, the first flight of a new design is not when the exciting or scary things happen. These events, if they occur, happen on later flights, when opening the speed, "G," or altitude envelopes.

The Quiver/Raptor 1 was designed to be an unmanned aircraft from the start. Since we at Scaled had actually designed and built the autopilot for Quiver, we were all a little apprehensive about trusting this plane to such a device. Burt decided it was too great a risk, and designed a "saddle" that was installed on top of the fuselage, much like a saddle on a horse. There was a rudimentary instrument panel, and a short, centrally mounted control stick that was mechanically connected to one aileron and one elevator. The only connection to the rudders was via a twist grip on the control stick, which used the same electric servos used by the autopilot, to move the rudders. There was also a switch so that the pilot, sitting externally astride the fuselage on the "saddle," could disconnect the ground controller and take over manual control.

I was the safety pilot on board the Quiver aircraft for Flight No. 10. The purpose of this flight was to evaluate the navigation mode, check a number of ground station software changes, and practice landings. Later, during a few low approaches, flown remotely by Dave Ganzer on the ground, I noted that the aircraft was not well-coordinated. I glanced back at the rudders and saw that both rudders were deployed to the left. On the third low approach, this condition was worse. When Dave applied power for the go-around, the plane made an uncoordinated, skidding left turn, which was very uncomfortable for the pilot. I asked Dave to apply full right rudder for a moment as I watched the rudders. Nothing happened, so I took over control of the aircraft, fully expecting this problem to go away. To my chagrin, it did not.

I found myself flying in a full-rudder, full-aileron, forward slip. I made several attempts to land at Mojave, but it was soon obvious this was not going to happen. I decided to try to fly to Rosamond Dry Lake, about 10 miles south of the Mojave airport. There was lots of room on the lakebed, and I would not be constrained to the narrow confines of a runway. My first thought was to climb high enough to be able to parachute safely off the back of the Quiver, but there was so much aerodynamic drag being generated by the forward slip, there was insufficient power available to be able to climb at all. I was very low, only about 200 feet above the ground, and it was really difficult making it over the low ridge between Mojave and the dry lake. I came close to losing control of the Quiver several times, and my mouth was so dry, I could hardly talk on the radio.

I eventually cleared the ridge and began my descent to the surface of the dry lake. Dave Ganzer and I had discussed the strong adverse yaw characteristics of the Quiver, and I prepared to use this tendency for the nose to slice initially in the opposite direction of the aileron input. I practiced this odd maneuver a couple of times as I approached the north edge of the lake. It worked far better than I had thought it would, and I was beginning to believe I had a chance of not only surviving this event, but possibly even saving the Quiver!

I flew down as close to the lakebed surface as I dared and then began to slow down for the landing. With full right aileron applied just to be able to fly, I was in a 35-degree right bank, and I watched my right wing tip getting very close to the dry lakebed. I gritted my teeth and brought the control stick from its full-right position all the way over to the full-left position. Strong adverse yaw caused the nose to slice to the right until the wings were level and she was perfectly aligned with her velocity vector. I simply reduced power to idle and set her down on the dry lake. I braked to a stop and was rather amazed to find that I was alive! It was such an anticlimax, but it was the closest call I have ever had. Even now, when I read my actual flight report of this incident, I still get cold shivers.

Ares Flutters

Flying Ares one day, I remember experiencing flutter of the elevators while opening the speed envelope in this single-engine jet fighter. It was the first time we had been over 300 knots indicated in Ares, and I was flying level at 15,000 feet when I hit some turbulence. Suddenly the stick began vibrating, and I could feel it strongly in the seat of my pants. I glanced over my left shoulder at the same time as I brought the power lever to hard idle as I pulled the plane into a vertical climb in an attempt to slow down as rapidly as possible. The elevators on the trailing edge of the canard were a blur! It seemed to take an age before this violent fluttering of the elevators quit, and while I was preparing to use the ejection seat when the vibration abruptly stopped. I pitched over and proceeded at very low speed to the airport for an uneventful landing.

The carbon skins had separated from the foam cores of the elevators. This may have saved the day, as the natural frequency of the elevators was changed by the skin separation, and this probably stopped the flutter. It turned out that the elevators were incorrectly balanced, and the sharp-edged turbulence was enough to start the elevators oscillating. Fortunately, this was not divergent flutter, which would have instantly ruined my day!

Push Forward to Land

During an early altitude envelope-expansion flight in the Proteus, my copilot, Pete Siebold, and I had an interesting experience. The pitch forces in Proteus are very high, and the pitch trim is a critically important item. The trim tab is not hinged at the trailing edge of the elevator as it is in most planes, but is mounted on two rather long booms that extend aft from the elevator's trailing edge about a foot. The airfoil-shaped trim tab is thus able to generate very large forces and provide hands-off, zero pitch forces to the pilot.

We were above 50,000 feet and evaluating pitch trim effectiveness while we slowed down. As I slowed to close to the stall speed, I was trimming to zero stick force, when suddenly there was a dramatic nose-down trim force. It took both of us to control this powerful tendency to pitch down, and neither of us was aware that the problem was caused by flow separation and thus a stalled pitch trim tab. I was frantically trimming the nose up to alleviate the nose-down force on the control sticks, but because the tab was already at such a high angle to the breeze, it had stalled, and this accomplished nothing. We decided that we should descend and return to base while we still had marginal control. Since we didn't have a chase up at this altitude, we were not able to tell if the trim tab had broken off or was still in position between its booms. I continued to move the trim switches in both directions, hoping the problem would cure itself.

We called for our Duchess chase to meet us as high as possible, and we began to descend gingerly. The stick forces were unbearably high at high speeds, so we had to descend at as slow an airspeed as possible. We finally got down low enough for the Duchess to look us over, and we were puzzled to hear that our pitch trim tab was in place and looked normal. We decided to land and check things out.

We had been pulling between 75 and 100 pounds on each stick, and we were both very tired. It is also difficult to fly with two pilots working two control sticks at the same time. We were very concerned about our ability to flare the plane to land. We turned final and began to slow for the landing. We were both still pulling on each stick with considerable force, when suddenly the airflow over the trim tab re-attached, and the tab suddenly became very effective, but in the opposite direction! On very short final, Pete and I went from pulling on the sticks to fly the glide slope, to pushing on each stick to prevent the nose from rising. I came to idle power, and we touched down fairly smoothly.

This was the first and only time I have ever had to push forward on a control stick to land! We discovered that the airfoil shape of this trim tab was not a good one for high altitude, and we subsequently designed and built a new airfoil, which has worked perfectly ever since.

Mach Limits

Another interesting and scary pitch-related event occurred in the Proteus; this time it was Mach related. My copilot, Mike Alsbury, and I were crossing the Pacific from Majuro in the Marshall Islands to Guam. We were at 54,000 feet in clear air. Slowly I became aware of a drop in indicated airspeed. I corrected with more power, but soon this was not enough. The indicated speed continued to decay. I descended to try to get the speed back, but we quickly realized this was not the problem. We had turned on pitot heat during our initial climb through a cloud layer, and it was still on. Yet we were experiencing classic pitot icing. The airspeed indicator needle continued to drop all the way down to where it normally would be when we are parked on the ramp. Now we were without any speed information, including our Mach indication since it is derived from the normal air-data boom, which was now frozen! As high as we were, our maximum speed limit is 0.61 Mach. This is a hard limit in Proteus because above this speed, the fat subsonic airfoils on the canard or forward wing shock up with transonic flow, and the canard loses lift, causing the nose to drop. This, of course, exacerbates the problem as this causes the speed to increase. A bad thing at any altitude, but especially bad up where we were.

I had seen this Mach effect before, during envelope expansion flight testing, and I explained to Mike what might happen as we requested a lower altitude from the Guam controller. We gingerly started our descent, but without an indicated airspeed or Mach number, we had no idea how fast we were going. Soon, there was a rumbling sound, which rapidly became a roaring noise literally as loud as a train going through the cabin! The nose dropped, and we both applied all the force we could muster to each control stick. This force was well in excess of 100 pounds on each control stick, and gradually, much too slowly for us, we pulled out of the resulting dive. The noise went away, and we both looked at each other in awe at the thought of what might have happened if we had not reacted as quickly as we did. We continued our descent at a much lower rate, and finally, after what seemed an inordinate amount of time, we were down low enough that we could no longer fly fast enough to exceed our Mach limit.

This was truly a scary event, and as we continue to operate Proteus in the upper atmosphere, we are very careful about Mach limits. The problem seems to have been ice crystals that are abundant at those altitudes in the tropics. Our pitot was a general, aviation-type, heated pitot, which while perfectly adequate at lower altitudes, was woefully inadequate up at 54,000 feet, where the outside air temperature reaches down to minus 100 degrees Fahrenheit. All it did was slightly melt these super-cooled ice crystals and cause them to stick together and eventually block up our pitot. Another valuable lesson learned!

Pressure Suit Training

Many interesting things have happened to me during my career as a test pilot for Burt Rutan, but one I really enjoyed was when my copilot and I traveled up to Beale Air Force Base in my Long-EZ, to undergo pressure suit training in preparation for flying as high as the Proteus would go. We were given a very thorough education on the physical problems of high altitude flight and the terrifying results if one were exposed to the atmosphere at or above 63,000 feet. This is known as the Armstrong Line, and this is where your blood begins to boil in your veins if you are exposed to the outside air. This line is also considered from a physical standpoint to be the beginning of space. There is very little pressure change from this altitude to the moon's surface.

We were then fitted into pressure suits, the same ones used by Air Force U-2 pilots. It takes two people to get you into one of these suits through a rather small, zippered opening in the back of the suit. After donning the helmet, gloves, and boots, I actually experienced a feeling of claustrophobia for a few seconds until I got used to the loud sound of my own breathing inside the helmet. We were then hooked up to a liquid oxygen supply and left reclining in chairs among several U-2 pilots, as Beale is a fully operational U-2 base. After breathing 100 percent oxygen for almost an hour to clear all of the nitrogen out of our blood, we were taken, one at a time, to a small, one-person altitude chamber. We were strapped into an ejection-like seat and left alone as the huge door was shut. There were thick glass windows, and we could see the doctor, who had given us the classroom training, as well as several helpers looking in at us as though we were lab rats. There was also an open container of water on the windowsill.

We were taken to 10,000 feet then back down to see if our ears were going to be OK; then we went through a series of altitude increases and could begin to see just how the suit worked and how it would protect us in the event of a rupture in our cabin. The most impressive event was when they showed us a rapid decompression from 25,000 to 75,000 feet in only a second or two!! It sounded and felt like an explosion, and the suit instantly inflated until it was as hard as a car tire. The water in the open container boiled almost out of the container! It was difficult but not impossible to move your arms and feet enough to fly a plane. I was extremely impressed and enjoyed every minute of this incredible training. It was a fabulous opportunity, and it gave me the confidence to proceed with our high-altitude testing in the Proteus.

Achievements

Later, in Mojave, the NASA pressure suit support ground crew got both of us into our pressure suits, and we climbed the Proteus to just above the Armstrong Line to set three U.S. National as well as World altitude records for the jet-powered 6,000-kilogram weight class. These records include absolute altitude attained: 63,245 feet; maximum altitude in level flight: 62,385 feet; and maximum altitude carrying a 1,000-kilogram payload: 55,994 feet.

This was, I thought, a tremendous achievement for a small company like Scaled Composites, a very large feather in Burt's cap, and a testament to the dedicated engineers and shop people who designed and fabricated this amazing aircraft. I have flown the Proteus across the Atlantic to the Paris Air Show. We have also crossed the Pacific to Hawaii, the Marshall Islands, Guam, Okinawa, and Japan. We have flown to Alaska and on to circle the North Pole. Proteus has also crossed the United States on several occasions. All of these flights had essentially zero problems.

At Scaled, Burt is always admonishing us to have FUN! I know I do!

Darn Simple Test Pilot
Tom Hill

Darn simple test pilot. That's how I consider myself most times. And there's good reason. I wasn't part of any of the spectacular aerospace programs of the 1990s. No F-22 testing in my logbook, and I watched on the sidelines as the C-17 was put through its paces when it was brand-new. I even knew people from my test pilot school class who were initial cadre for the C-130 program. There were still a lot of new aircraft being developed and flown in those days; although, perhaps not as much as during the "Golden Age of Flight Test." I, however, didn't do any of that sexy, cutting-edge, envelope-expansion-type flying. I wasn't that lucky. Generally, I was a simple guy doing simple stuff.

The greater part of my testing at Edwards Air Force Base was boring holes in the sky with the F-15. While it sounds exciting, it was mostly software testing. Today's technological aircraft systems are supposed to be easier and quicker to update; however, we all know they definitely aren't. But, that's another story. Anyway, I have dozens of hours droning up and down an infamous little dirt road at Edwards playing the monkey. I say "monkey" because most software testing is essentially pressing buttons in specific sequences and has little to do with being a steely-eyed Tactical Air Command fighter pilot or a highly trained, golden-armed United States Air Force Test Pilot School graduate. It is completely about doing complex, repetitive tasks and making your handler—the test conductor—happy. In fact, if you do things really well, you might be given a lollipop at the end of the day. (Sure sounds like being a monkey to me!)

The stuff we did on Cords Road—that infamous dirt road—was tasking. I remember coming back from a 2.5-hour mission absolutely exhausted. Normally these missions included over 20 test passes and cards, coordinating five or six test targets, and making sure you didn't turn the wrong thing on at the wrong time. Basically anything to work your back-end off. It was both physically and mentally arduous. If you've never experienced something like this, imagine being strapped to the seat in your car for four or five hours straight, unable to move, while simultaneously coordinating a large, outdoor wedding at your house. Suppose it's raining. Now, what do you think? While not particularly challenging, it was usually one crisis after another. Still, none of this chaos was especially dangerous. We *weren't* stretching the envelope. The airplane *wasn't* going anywhere it hadn't been before. Fairly "cheesy" test pilot stuff. Definitely not the stuff of legends.

Before you start feeling too sorry for me, I was involved with one program that, for a short period, was totally about envelope expansion. It had all the trimmings of one of the major packages. Yet this other program almost doesn't count because it was so small. It involved an aircraft that was the antithesis of the sexy F-15. What can possibly be the opposite of the F-15? Well, how does a twin-engine motor-glider sound? Before you screw your face into contortions trying to figure out what a twin-engine motor-glider looks like, imagine a Cessna Skymaster configured with a really long, low wing, and you've got the picture. It was a pusher/puller built by Schweitzer Aircraft Company that was based on one of their popular gliders. The airplane was designed as a long-duration, covert-surveillance aircraft for the U.S. Coast Guard. Although it was designed for the military it required the same certification efforts of any new, civilian-registered airplane. Like I said, it had all the ingredients of a major flight test program, topped off with all the heartache and pain, but without the glory of most military flight test programs. At first it was called the RG-8 Twin but was soon renamed the RU-38.

I was invited into this program after graduating from Test Pilot School, mostly because the F-15 flight testing was at a lull, and this tiny program needed help—more like man power. Soon after being introduced to the project, I coined the phrase "the agricultural approach to flight test" to describe the program's characteristics. While the United State Air Force Test Pilot School is world-famous for training pilots and engineers to tackle high-technology, high-risk flight test programs, I was wholly unprepared for the "back of the napkin … kick the tires … that feels right" kind of flight test that characterized this program. The entire project reminded me of stories that I had read about aircraft testing in WWII. We didn't enjoy the resources of the larger programs, and therefore, we had to depend on the savvy and smarts of our own test team to get things done. While nothing we did was particularly dangerous, we had to shoulder the responsibility for anything that went wrong. Although we were unable to blame anyone else for project mishaps, we were able to accept full credit for our successes. Also our team consisted of a mere dozen people. As I like to say, "It was small enough to see the beginning, end, and all sides." Like I said, it wasn't your standard Air Force test program.

Did I already mention that everything to do with this program was low budget? I'll give you an example. After two years of wrangling, redesigning, and tackling programmatic issues, we were finally prepared for the first flight of our entirely reworked RU-38. I was the sole "legacy" on the team; all of the other team members were brand-new. On the big day, we went to Elmira, New York, to see just what our plane could do.

Like any first flight, we had to run through several high-speed taxi tests before the real flight. Remember, we're talking about a heavyweight glider, so the maximum taxi speed was about 50 knots. Our rental van didn't have any problems keeping up with the plane as it rolled down the runway.

While I drove the van, one of our new engineers planned to film the whole event through the open passenger window. Actually, I think he planned to stick his head out the window like somebody's pet. My buddy, Nils Larson, the new project pilot and test manager, was at the RU-38's controls. He would be leading the parade of vehicles (his aircraft and our van) to the runway. After a few run-up checks of the newly regeared engines, he positioned himself on the runway with tower's permission. We positioned ourselves slightly aft for ideal footage. Brian, the new engineer and designated videographer, got his camera ready.

Time for takeoff! Brian filmed every second of the engines' acceleration as they roared to life. The vibration from two Continental 550s was obvious in our chase car. The sound was deafening. Nils' experience in the aircraft must have been awesome. After being satisfied that all was well with his engine instruments, Nils released the brakes, and the RU-38 shot away, leaving me in the dust. So, here I am, a big-shot test pilot with one duty in life—driving in a good chase position—*and* I'm being left behind. I floored the accelerator with Brian hanging his cranium, shoulders, and most of his upper body out of the window trying to keep the RU-38 in his camera's field of view. We closed the gap, getting to where we were supposed to be from the beginning. Brian filmed the whole way as his body took the full force of the 70-mile-an-hour wind. His hair was flapping in the wind, cheeks pushed in, body pushed around. OK, we were military dudes so not a lot of hair was flapping in the wind; still, Brian struggled to keep things in view. As quickly as it had begun, the high-speed taxi was over. Nils reached his maximum speed and promptly decelerated. Everything looked wonderful.

Brian captured the whole event from start to finish, and when he finally pulled his body back into the van, his cranium had a cool, wind-swept look. You know, the look you get from riding the roller coasters too many times in a row. So, Brian is back in the van, obviously proud of his photography skills, when he begins to stare right at me, blinking profusely.

"What's up with you?" I said.

"I think I lost a contact," blink, blink, blink.

Apparently, his contact was the victim of "playing the dog-hanging-out-the-window" trick and was swept away by the wind during the test run. After a short, fruitless search, we gave up any hope of finding it. Oh well, casualty of war.

The following day, Nils made his first flight. While it was much more interesting than any flight deserved to be, I'll leave it to Nils to tell that story.

I will, however, describe one of the most exciting events anyone had in the RU-38 program. In fact, it was one of the most exciting events during my Air Force career, but first I need to give you some background. The airplane was originally fashioned from the parts of a single-engine RG-8. That aircraft's tail was chopped off, and the width of the remaining fuselage was widened 18 inches. A pusher engine was added, and then a boom tail (like the one on the P-38) was installed. Finally, the taildragger landing gear was eliminated in favor of a tricycle gear. The amazing thing was that this configuration was termed a "modification" of the original RG-8. The entire aircraft weighed over 6,000 pounds and was using a wing originally designed to withstand a 600- to 1,000-pound aircraft. There was no way this aircraft should have been compared to the RG-8. It was considerably different and deserved its own identity.

The original designers totally underestimated the aircraft's drag. The two Continental RO 550s that were originally installed were completely insufficient to get the aircraft to its limiting airspeed in level flight. Shoot, you needed a 30-degree dive before the aircraft would begin to accelerate. We were told by the designers before the first flight to "watch out and to avoid overspeeding the aircraft, because with the two huge engines, it is clearly overpowered." While the aircraft had a lot of power—two engines producing over 310 horsepower each—it was like flying a brick wall. There was so much drag, parasitic and induced, that the possibility of unintentional overspeeds was laughable. This was a considerable challenge when collecting flutter data. We had to fly five or six thousand feet above the desired test conditions, push the power up to maximum, lower the nose to 30 degrees, and hope for the best as the airspeed crept up. Then, *maybe* we had enough altitude to reach the desired conditions before descending too low. Nope, the RU-38 was no speed demon.

I flew with a company pilot on the day of my story. We were trying to reach the high-speed record for the aircraft—a whopping 167 knots. This test point was funny, when you consider my other aircraft was the 2.5 Mach F-15 Eagle. The world is an ironic place. Anyway, the first difference you would have noticed between the pilots trained at military test pilot school and the "on the job" trained pilots associated with this program were their assessment of what was considered dangerous, and their resulting risk-reduction procedures. If it had not been for our safety paperwork, the military guys would have been flying the RU-38 equipped with a standard helmet, visor down, while the company guys would have been out there without so much as a baseball cap. I routinely wore my helmet, suffering from daily "helmet head"—while the company guys looked as if they were on a Sunday outing whenever they flew. Since this test point was high-risk, both of us were wearing our helmets. A fortunate occurrence considering what was about to happen.

As briefed, I took the aircraft to 13,000 feet to begin the wild dive toward the high-speed point. We had already flown to a couple of other speeds as a buildup to the final end point. Heading toward the field, I lowered the nose and pushed the throttles to maximum. More and more forward pressure was needed on the stick to keep the nose from rising; the aircraft couldn't be trimmed at those speeds.

We raced through 120 …130 … 140 knots. The aircraft's drag began to slow things down. The noise was incredible. Even with my earplugs and helmet, I could barely hear myself think, let alone my partner's speed calls

145 … 150 the altitude was winding away a lot faster than the speed was building up. It was beginning to look questionable if we'd get to the test conditions before the abort altitude.

… 155 … 160 the stick was now very forward and a bit twitchy. I was making very deliberate and subtle control inputs to avoid over-controlling the airplane. The altitude was running away, but the airspeed was almost there

165—we're almost there—166 …

What's happening to the windscreen? Just as we reached our maximum speed, my windscreen began to bow in a couple of inches at the base, just above the engine cowling. It looked just like the view from inside an oilcan when you dimple the outside—slightly caved in. Jeeez! Now there's something you don't see every day! I pulled the throttles, slowly let the nose rise, and shouted over the noise to my partner, "Hey, check out my windscreen."

Not wanting to disturb anything by taking too abrupt an action, I slowly recovered the aircraft to level flight. Without gravity forcing the aircraft forward, our speed dropped, and the controls began to feel more normal. Passing through 150 knots, the dimple in my windscreen pushed out with a "pop!" Everything else about the sortie was uneventful through the landing. In the end, I definitely knew that we had been to the aircraft's limit.

That test point was my last major contribution to the RU-38 program. Not long after this, the program "stood down" for over two years, so aircraft and program improvements could be implemented. During this time, I was relegated to other duties and projects in the F-15.

I'll never forget that windscreen caving in, or that I treated the event so nonchalantly when it happened. While none of this is particularly noteworthy compared to a high-tech, advanced test program like the F-22, it sure is significant to me. Even if the aircraft is completely forgotten, I'll always remember its importance to me. It showed me that anything can happen in a flight test. And, it usually does ... even to darn simple test pilots.

BEING THE FIRST

The aeroplane will never fly.

-Lord Haldane
Minister of War
Britain, 1907

Docking with Space Station Mir
Charlie Precourt

It was my fortieth birthday, and I couldn't have dreamed of a better way to celebrate. I was hurtling through space at a speed of over five miles per second on board the Space Shuttle Atlantis, headed for a rendezvous with the Russian Space Station Mir! This was to be the first ever docking using the space shuttle, and our first join-up in space with the Russians since Apollo-Soyuz twenty years earlier. I awoke from our second night's sleep on orbit to a surprise birthday party that my crew had arranged for breakfast—*including* an inflatable cake. There wouldn't be time the rest of the day to think about anything but the task ahead, so they had my party early! The final stages of the rendezvous would take literally the entire day. Thinking back on it now, I often wonder if I hadn't dreamt the whole birthday thing. That is until I look at the photos Ellen Baker, one of our mission specialists, shot as I pretended to "blow out" the candles on the "cake" while it floated weightless in front of me.

Life has been exciting in the astronaut corps the past few years. When I joined the space program in 1990 we were flying shuttles with primarily U.S. mission objectives and U.S. crews. But in 1991, Presidents Bush and Gorbachev signed an agreement to open an exchange program between our space agencies, including the flight of a cosmonaut on the shuttle and an American on Mir. Since that time, the halls of the astronaut corps look more like the United Nations than an office in Houston, Texas. Astronauts from over a dozen countries (speaking as many languages) began to train in Houston for the assembly of the new International Space Station.

In March 1995, Norm Thagard became the first American to launch on a Russian rocket when he and his two Russian crewmates

181

left Kazakhstan in their Soyuz for a three-month mission to Mir. Our job on Atlantis was to bring the Mir's replacement crew, two Russian cosmonauts, Anatoly Soloviev and Nikolai Budarin. Nikolai was a rookie, and he never would have thought his first launch to space would be on an American shuttle!

The Atlantis crew came together in the fall of 1994 to begin developing the flight plan. Hoot Gibson, the mission commander, asked me to be his pilot for the flight. We had Greg Harbaugh as our lead flight engineer, and Ellen Baker and Bonnie Dunbar as the other mission specialists. Bonnie had been training as Norm's backup in Russia, and now that he was in space, she joined Atlantis to be part of the science mission we planned for the spacelab module in our payload bay. Norm was the first American to spend more than two weeks in space since the Skylab missions of the 1970s. The science community was jumping over the prospects of getting their hands on him for medical data when we arrived at Mir. Ellen and Bonnie coordinated the science aspects of the flight, while Hoot, Greg, and I worked out the rendezvous and docking details as well as the usual ascent and entry control of the shuttle orbiter. It was turning out to be the most challenging shuttle mission in years; adding the Russian dimension made it even better.

I'll never forget the first visit that our cosmonaut crewmates made to Houston. We arranged a weekend social to get to know each other and decided to drive to Galveston to give them a tour of the coast, beaches, and "old town" sights. The only problem was, they didn't speak English, *and* we couldn't speak Russian. We had begun to study Russian in classes with a teacher from the Defense Language Institute who came to Houston to work with us. Our capability was pretty pathetic. I remember driving Nikolai in my pickup truck with an English-Russian dictionary as our only translator. It took almost the entire drive to Galveston to figure out that we were both married and had kids in school! I thought it would be a shame if we couldn't communicate enough to at least "share a moment" in space while looking at the beautiful earth from a shuttle window. I became determined that I'd learn some Russian in the next eight months. That turned out to be as big a challenge as flying the mission itself!

The Space Shuttle Atlantis didn't have the hardware necessary to dock with Mir when we started this venture. As a matter of fact, it didn't have docking hardware for any space station. So, when the negotiations for this exchange program were finalized, the program managers started the process to design and build hardware that would adapt to the shuttle and the Mir to allow the docking. The Russians provided a docking mechanism, which we affixed to the top of a shuttle airlock module. This section would then be placed into the payload bay of the shuttle orbiter, approximately midway down the tunnel that normally joins the Spacelab with the cockpit end of the ship. The idea was that as the astronauts and cosmonauts floated down the tunnel they could turn vertical and head into the Mir once we were docked, or they could keep going straight and end up in the lab.

The Russian mechanism was known as the Androgynous Peripheral Docking Mechanism, or APDS. Although much evolved and modified for this new application, it was actually a holdover from the Apollo-Soyuz docking mechanism built in 1975. It was called androgynous because it was not a male-to-female mating design like most joining hardware. The folklore goes something like this: neither the Soviet Union nor the United States would stand for a male-female docking mechanism because no one could agree which country would get which half! Therefore, the mechanism was designed to be identical on both sides of the interface. It consists of three equally spaced petals that are positioned around the circumference of the docking ring. The spaces between each petal mesh with the petals of the other spacecraft's docking mechanism, whose petals are placed in a complimentary fashion—like the fingers of your left and right hands overlapping when you fold your hands together.

This mechanism was the key design modification we needed to be able to complete a docking mission with the space shuttle. The APDS was designed by Russian engineer, Dr. Syromyatnikov; the same engineer who designed the docking mechanism for Apollo-Soyuz. It was a fairly simple concept, but when you looked at its inner workings, you came away with the impression that it was like a Swiss watch. It was a complex mechanism that not only had to allow the two ships to hook together, but also had to have shock absorbers to take up the loads of contact (two ships each a quarter of a million pounds coming together while flying in formation at 17,500 miles per hour). In addition, it had to be able to pull the two halves into a hard mate that would provide a pressure seal while allowing for hatches inside the mechanism to be opened once docked, so that crew and cargo could pass between the ships during the docked phase of the flight. The space shuttle was considered the active vehicle. It would maneuver to align itself with the passive Mir Station, which was to be held steady for us during the docking. Therefore, the docking mechanism would be operated by the shuttle crew through a Russian control panel installed in our cockpit. With all of this Russian hardware being added to Atlantis, we had to travel to Moscow a few times to learn how to use it.

We went to Moscow for our first two-week visit in October 1994 and were given a grand tour of the Russian Space Agency facilities. It was pure culture shock. We visited Energia Rocket Corporation and Khrunichev, where all the Soviet rockets had been built. We toured the Moscow flight control center and went to Star City, the Gagarin Cosmonaut Training Center, for training on the Mir Station systems. From Dr. Syromyatnikov, we received quite a history lesson about how the Apollo-Soyuz was put together on the Soviet side. He not only showed us a functional mockup of the docking mechanism we would fly, but trained us to operate it with the same type of control panels that were being installed in the Atlantis. We ran through a series of failure cases until we were comfortable with his system. It was a special honor to be receiving instruction directly from the original designer.

Back in Houston, we were feverishly developing simulations that would allow us to practice the docking while simultaneously fine-tuning the techniques we'd need to use in space. Hoot, Greg, and I spent hundreds of hours in the simulators developing the plan that would bring us to a successful docking. The challenge of this task was to launch the Atlantis within five minutes of a predetermined time, then bring it and the Mir into contact within two minutes of another predetermined time while over Russian territory, and with a relative closing velocity between .07 and .13 feet per second (really slow!)

with no more than two degrees or three inches of displacement off center between the two docking mechanisms. Needless to say, we had to work with many variables to prevent damaging either the shuttle or the Mir when the two came into contact. To complicate matters, the Russians didn't have continuous satellite communications with Mir, they wanted us to dock over Russian territory so they could send telemetry and commands as needed directly to the station during the whole event.

In order to handle all of these constraints, we had developed a set of specialized "tools" to guide us through the rendezvous. We added a laser range finder to the payload bay. This addition would supplement our onboard radar system with distance and speed information when approaching the station. Also, we had a trajectory display on a laptop computer that plotted our relative position during the approach. For redundancy, we had a hand-held laser that was like a traffic cop's radar gun, several optical sights, and remote-mounted viewing cameras. Special docking targets were assigned to make sure that the two ships were aligned within tolerances before we brought them into contact. We called this an "eight-dimensional problem" because, in order to pull this off, we had to simultaneously control eight parameters while flying the shuttle. We had to control: roll, pitch, and yaw of the shuttle relative to the station; position left-right, up-down, and in-out relative to the station; as well as, speed at contact and time of contact. We had our hands full!

Once on orbit (and with the birthday party out of the way), we had to get to work. Several orbit burners needed to be continually adjusted in order to move our orbit into synch with Mir's. (This rendezvous stuff is really quite interesting.) Orbital mechanics can be complicated, but the big picture is fairly simple. If a spacecraft is in orbit, its flight path traces a hoop orbit that is fixed in space and the earth turns underneath it. The rendezvous trick is to get into the same hoop as the target. However, since the earth is rotating you can't just launch whenever you want. Your hoop (orbit) may not necessarily be parallel with the target orbit. Instead, the two hoops may be crossing at sharp angles, making it impossible for the two spacecraft to link up.

The first task our team had for the rendezvous was to launch at the right time. In this case, at the time of day when Cape Kennedy passed directly underneath Mir's orbit making it possible for us to jump into their hoop. On June 27, 1995, we had a seven-minute launch window when this would work. We got lucky with the weather and lifted off spot on time, and entered an orbit beneath Mir that was initially 85 miles altitude at the low point (perigee) of the orbit, and 160 miles high at the peak (apogee). This put us in an elliptical orbit below Mir to begin the chase.

The launch is truly impressive. The main engines light at six seconds before liftoff and send a tremor through out the ship. Then, during booster ignition, it is simultaneously like an explosion and a giant push in the back as we leave the pad. The first stage on the solid rockets is quite rough and turbulent. The gravitational forces build to a bit less than three positive G's just before booster burnout. Since we're on our backs, we feel the G's as acceleration through the chest, a phenomenon described as "a gorilla sitting on your chest." We drop the boosters, and suddenly it's quiet and smooth, but the thrust is still there pushing like "electric drive." Gradually, as we lose fuel weight, the G's build back up to three again, and we throttle the engines to stay at 3G's until the main engine cutoff. This protects the structure from overstress. When we cut off the engines, it's instantaneous zero-G, and everything becomes absolutely quiet and anything not secure floats. Unbelievable!

The second trick of a rendezvous is to catch up to the target. By being at a lower altitude, we circle the earth faster than the Mir. This is like being on the inside lane of a racetrack. We have a bit less distance to travel with each orbit, so we gradually start catching up to the guy in the outside lane. As we catch up, we have to gradually raise our orbit to slow the approach speed and park ourselves in the same orbit, yet slightly behind, where we can maneuver in manually for the docking. Hoot, Greg, and I performed six orbit-adjust burns during the first two days of the mission to ease in behind the Mir. Now thirty-eight hours into the mission, we are closing from a range of eight miles behind, and we have a beautiful view of the Mir ahead. (Our first sighting was from longer range, where it appeared as a star.) Now we could make out the individual modules. It was hard to believe that *this* was the outpost where people had been living continuously for the last seven years!

From this range, we would be computing all of the remaining adjustment burns using our on-board sensors only. Up until now the ground crew had assisted us using their tracking information on the two spacecraft. As we closed our sensors became the most effective tool for the rendezvous. We locked on the radar and attempted to get laser data … but no luck. Greg was trying to get the hand-held laser to work—but it was dead. We went to the backup, and ditto. Both were dead. There wasn't any power getting to the unit. Greg shot down to the tool cabinet and grabbed a screwdriver to open the case. What a surprise to find the batteries had never been packed—for *either* unit! The units required special batteries that we would learn later had been removed for shipment and never reinstalled. Time to improvise! We pulled out the power adapter, known as the "break-out box," which allows us to plug into the orbiter outlets and get 28 volts DC. From there, the break-out box can adjust the voltage to what is needed for the laser units. We "hot wired" them to the battery terminals inside the case. Presto! We've got power! Greg goes to the window and starts "lasing" the station for range and range-rate data, while I'm using the trajectory monitoring displays to give Hoot adjustment corrections to "burn" with the hand controllers. We're in business, pulling in underneath the Mir at a range of 2,650 feet and closing at 7 feet per second. It is time to start slowing down. Hoot makes a few impulses through the hand controller, and I verify the trajectory change on the display. Greg reads out the new range and closure rate that confirms we're tracking exactly where we want to be.

The final trick was to time the arrival so as to be over Russia when contact occurs. I set up a timing card that followed our range-to-target against a set of preplanned milestones. We'd be able to tell if we were early or late from this information. Also, I could transmit more corrections for Hoot to make as he kept us in the approach corridor while flying formation out the window. Since firing our thrusters directly at Mir would damage the delicate solar arrays that produced the electrical power for the station; we turned the shuttle's jets to a special mode when we were 1000 feet away. Our thrusters were limited to those that were angled to the side, and unfortunately, this made our control less precise. All of the time in the simulator paid off as we managed to keep Atlantis right on the timeline. At 450 feet, the Mir maneuvered to point its docking port towards us. They passively continued to hold this position during docking. Coming into the 270-foot range, we entered "station keeping," to synchronize the final approach with Moscow. For docking, we pushed closer to Mir at precisely 38 minutes to contact from 270 feet using a closure rate of one-half of one foot per second. This is very slow, but if we were going too fast at this point in the ball game, things could get out of hand in a real hurry. With 170 feet to go, we were down to one-tenth of a foot per second closure, and we would hold that all the way to contact. We were working our way ever closer now, and for the first time, we could see the faces of the Mir crew in the station's windows. I wanted to call on the radio for them to "lower their arms and stand by to be boarded," but thought better of it. That is until we saw Norm's face—then we asked him how much it was worth to him for us to come in and bring him home! He would have paid us a year's salary by this time. He had been at the station for over one hundred days and was more than ready to go home.

At the 30-foot range, we felt like we were tucked in right along side, and we didn't dare breathe lest we get some unwanted relative motion. Unbelievable—two spacecraft, weighing a quarter of a million pounds each, in tight formation, 206 nautical miles above the south Atlantic, racing north toward Moscow at 17,500 miles per hour! At this range we had to read the visual docking target inside the Mir docking mechanism to judge the relative angles of alignment between the two ships. If the cross of the target were not superimposed over the centerlines of the back plate the target was mounted to, then it would indicate we were off axis. We would have to rotate the orbiter in pitch, roll, or yaw to compensate, otherwise the docking mechanisms wouldn't mate. Because the instructors never would give us a "normal" day in training, we had practiced this frequently in the simulator. Today, we had nailed it to less than three-tenths of a degree, well within the two degrees we were allowed.

During training, I had been curious about the actual sensation of physical contact during docking. You can simulate a lot of things, but mechanical contact between two ships of this size is not one of them. As we counted down to contact from three feet, we waited in anticipation for the mechanism to penetrate the Mir docking port. We were spring-loaded for the "back-away" maneuver (we had trained heavily in the simulator for this event) should the mechanisms fail to latch. As we passed two inches prior to contact, we fired a set of thrusters to nudge us into place. We felt Atlantis edge into contact, which gave a pleasant mechanical vibration followed by a firm "Capture" light on our docking panel. We had nailed it!

Our contact conditions were nearly perfect. We arrived a mere two seconds past the predetermined time, with an exact velocity of 0.1 feet per second, and less than an inch of displacement from dead center. There was quite a celebration as we watched the mechanism run through its paces to draw the two vehicles into hard mate. Norm and his cosmonaut crewmates were going home!

Once the docking was complete, Greg ran through the remaining procedures to pressurize the volume between the two hatches. We hurriedly set about getting ready to open the hatches in preparation for the handshake in space between Russians and Americans—the first time since Apollo-Soyuz in 1975. I went to the hatch while we were awaiting the final pressurization. I peeked through the window and saw Norm and Volodya floating in their side of the docking compartment. They were grinning from ear-to-ear and doing summersaults in the weightlessness. Gennady was in the background filming the whole thing. I rapped on the window and got Voldya's attention. He floated over and asked with a grin what we were waiting for … "Get your hatch open!"

When we had all our cameras ready, we opened the final hatch to Mir. Looking inside there was a moment of silence … followed by, "Hey, you're upside down!"

Then from their side, "No, you're upside down!"

We had not anticipated the orientation differences between the two ships, and it turned out that when docked, our floor was their ceiling. Of course, in weightlessness that is not really a problem, but it made for amusing first words between our crews. Then it was bedlam. There were ten of us, and we had a great reunion in space. For the next couple of hours, we toured each other's spacecraft, and then made a television downlink to the control centers to celebrate with our ground control teams the first shuttle docking to Mir.

Now that we'd been through the long rendezvous process, it was time to adjust to a new phase of the flight. We were now a cargo ship ready to off load supplies and pick up return equipment for the journey home. We would spend the next three days loading literally over a ton of "stuff" back and forth across the hatches. At one point we had a "fur-ball" of activity in the main module of the Mir (we called it the "base" block). Since he had a lot of catching up to do, Volodya was going through a handover and outline with Anatoly. Volodya would soon be taking over the command of Mir. As we went floating by him in a pile of bodies and equipment, he did an inverted roll, looked at us with a grin, and said, "Urugan pashol," the hurricane is blowing through!

One of the more amazing things we did while docked was to bring home an entire avionics suite from Mir. A few weeks before our arrival, they docked a new module to their station by remote control. The avionics that they used are "recyclable," so they asked us to bring them home. The space shuttle is the only spacecraft in existence that has the ability to bring stuff like this back from space. It was a bonus for the Russians, who normally would not be able to reuse these boxes. So when Gennady and Volodya were in the module, they were literally floating in a sea of black boxes. There must have been 50 boxes floating free, and they were trying to read the serial numbers on each and check them against an inventory Moscow had sent. What a nightmare. Hoot and I discussed the probability of getting all this stuff "in the box" by the time we had to undock. We decided that I had better drop my planned activities and help them pack these avionics safely inside our spacelab module in the shuttle. Pandemonium would have been an understatement—but we made it.

We had a lot to do in order to transfer control of the Mir from Norm's crew to Anatoly and Nikolai, whom we would be leaving behind. This was Nikolai's first flight, and he was having a grand time. He had done well onboard the shuttle and was now deeply engaged in learning his responsibilities on Mir. Meanwhile, we pulled Norm, Gennady, and Volodya over to the shuttle's spacelab for "physicals." This was a unique opportunity for our scientists to examine the long-term effects of weightlessness and space travel on the human body. By the third day, the crew was getting a bit worn down. At one point, I remember floating back into the lab with some boxes to stow for the return trip and found that Gennady was free-floating in a corner, sound asleep! And this in spite of the noise Volodya was making on the treadmill. These guys were ready to go home.

While all of this was happening on orbit, there must have been some pretty happy folks on earth. The night before we were scheduled to undock, we received a message that they wanted us to do a "flying" photo-shoot using the Mir, Soyuz, and Atlantis simultaneously! Normally, the Soyuz capsule is docked to the side of Mir as an escape vehicle. The tiny capsule holds three in a cozy, side-by-side arrangement. There would be eight of us on the shuttle for the return trip and only two left on Mir. Much to our amazement, the ground teams had worked out a plan for us to close the hatches between the shuttle and Mir. Anatoly and Nikolai would get in the Soyuz and be the first craft to detach from the Mir. Then they would fly to a point approximately 100 feet off our wing and film us as we undocked the Atlantis. During all of this time the Mir would be empty.

Although the Russians had, in the past, left Mir temporarily empty while on fly-arounds with the Soyuz, this would be the first time they had done so in the proximity of the shuttle that was nearly as large as the station. Normally, the Russians would do this when they needed to reposition the Soyuz to provide an open docking port for a visiting cargo ship. However, the act of having three ships in formation in space (known as a "three-body problem) is not a simple matter. The control center faxed the procedure to us the night before undocking. It was some forty pages of new stuff that we had never simulated. We pulled out our procedure books, made the page changes from the uplinked fax, and started reviewing the plan. All seemed straightforward, although a bit complicated. We were ready to go with the new plan the following morning.

"Undocking Day" was here! Anatoly and Nikolai came across the hatch to the shuttle one last time, and we gave them some tortilla shells and other American foods and snacks that we knew they liked. We said our goodbyes, closed the hatches, and started to vent the air from between them so we could undock. Everyone moved into position. As I turned back, I saw Nikolai looking across the void of space through the Mir window, eating a tortilla and waving it at us! Then, he and Anatoly scurried off to the Soyuz to get ready to fly it away from the space station. Anatoly would be at the controls, and Nikolai at the Soyuz window with the video and still cameras ready to capture the image of our shuttle undocking from Mir. In the end, this film turned out to be some of the most impressive footage ever shot in spaceflight, but not without some intervening tense moments.

As the time countdown began, we had our cameras rolling inside the shuttle to film Anatoly. The little capsule backed away. They yawed to the north and slowly came to their station keeping point, just off our left wing. The Soyuz looked like a little gnat out there 100 feet away. We could see Anatoly firing thrusters from time to time to hold position. The exhaust plume of each jet firing reflected in the sun like water spray from a garden hose. It was really stunning against a backdrop of the vast blackness of space and the blue horizon of the earth. It was amazing to watch the Soyuz hold position.

We geared up the shuttle systems and started the sequence to open our latches and back away. Mir was empty, but we were holding it and the shuttle in position together using the Atlantis guidance and control systems. When we undocked, the Mir would be in "position-hold" on autopilot, which would allow Anatoly and Nikolai to redock the Soyuz. All went well with our initial separation, and we backed away to around 100 feet. We were to begin a fly-around at the 700 foot range. (Basically a loop over the top of the station and back underneath, for a total of one and a half revolutions.) Hoot transferred control of Atlantis over to me part way through the maneuver, but there was more excitement for Anatoly on board the Soyuz. Mir's central computer went down, and the station began to lose attitude control. It was beginning to drift freely as sunset was approaching. Anatoly was directed by Moscow to redock immediately. We looked on in amazement from the shuttle as he moved between the Mir and us and yawed around to line up with the docking port. Not two minutes before it started to get dark, Anatoly had successfully redocked to the Mir while it drifted, resulting in his having to hit a moving target. Had he not succeeded, both he and Nikolai may have been headed back to Earth before us!

We completed our fly-around loops of the Mir, photographing as much of the station as possible so that engineers on the ground could analyze the condition of various materials on the structure and how well they had stood up to the space environment. Keeping in position at 700 feet as we flew the loop; I would occasionally fire a thruster with the hand controller, which resulted in a "thumping" noise and a sudden, small lurch of the shuttle. (As I floated before the controls, it was as if the shuttle surges a few inches away from my grasp with the acceleration from each firing.)

It was time to pack up the rest of the shuttle and get ready to re-enter in two days. We had a special VHF radio for communicating with Mir that had been plugged in below deck. Now that we were moving away from the station, I elected to move it up to the flight deck in an attempt to consolidate stowage space. I was unaware, however, that the flight deck outlet, into which I had plugged the radio, was not rated for the surge current the radio needed to power up. I ended up blowing a fuse. I radioed the ground for an analysis. They asked me to pull out the volt-ohm meter to help troubleshoot the system. I was alone on the flight deck checking connector pins for voltage readings and hadn't noticed Volodya float up behind me. (He always had a knack for practical jokes, and I was usually a prime target.) Here I was about to make contact with the probes of the voltmeter to a couple of connector pins, when he makes a loud "phhhhhht" sound in my ear, imitating the noise that a sparking short circuit makes. He scared the living daylights out of me, and I tumbled backward from the panel to see his face grinning ear-to-ear as he watched me recover from my "mini" heart attack. I could have killed him! As it turns out, that was the start of a long friendship that we have shared ever since.

With the orbiter packed for landing, we got Norm and his cosmonaut crewmates suited up, and strapped into some specially-built, reclining seats that had been installed in the middeck of the shuttle. After three and a half months at zero-G, this would make their readaptation to gravity more comfortable. Many astronauts have said that they feel as if they are "plastered to the floor" when reentering gravity after several months of flight in weightlessness. Being reclined makes the stress much more bearable.

Hoot and I had the orbiter on the planned trajectory approaching Florida. Out of Mach 17 in a left bank coming up over the Yucatan Peninsula and then a reverse back to the right as we pass over Cuba around Mach 7. Coming down below 100,000 feet and hitting the west coast of Florida, we were still moving like gangbusters. Mach 5, and it looked like we'd be in Bermuda before we could get it down. But, as the shuttle slows down the descent angle becomes continually steeper. Before we knew it, we were over Kennedy at 45,000 feet—slowing through the speed of sound and starting our turn to align with runway 15. High final at 12,000 feet, 7 miles from the runway, 300 knots, descent angle at 20 degrees. At 3,000 feet I arm the landing gear for deploy; and at 2,000 feet, Hoot starts a preflare to shallow our descent. We have been coming down in excess of 12,000 feet per minute. It was time to intercept the inner, shallow glidepath for the last 400 feet to touchdown. I extend the gear at 300 feet, and Hoot sets it down at 200 knots, right as planned. I deploy the drag chute and we roll to a stop. Onboard, the first returning crew from a space station are safely home!

What an incredible mission! During our stay on orbit, we filmed several sequences that became part of the IMAX movie "Mission to Mir" that can be seen in many of the IMAX theaters around the country. Those images are as close to being there as any of us could create, but no film completely replicates the reality of being in space. In addition, we set a pair of records during the mission that were acknowledged by the Federation Aeronautique Internationale (FAI) and the National Aeronautic Association (NAA). The first record was for maximum altitude while linked for two or more spacecraft at 416 kilometers. Our flight broke the previous record established by the Apollo-Soyuz Mission. The second record was for absolute mass of spacecraft linked in flight at 209,000 kilograms.

This first docking of the American Space Shuttle Atlantis to the Russian Space Station Mir was the result of a tremendous effort by a great number of engineers and specialists in both Russia and the United States. The Atlantis and Mir crews are grateful for the efforts of these teams, and we remain in awe of how quickly we moved from enemies of the Cold War to cooperating partners in space. Today, Russia and the United States are partnered with the space agencies of Europe, Canada, and Japan, building the International Space Station. The lessons learned during this and subsequent Mir dockings have given these agencies invaluable data for future endeavors. Stay tuned for more great adventures in space!

Around at Last
Bertrand Piccard

High above the red vastness of the Sahara, the silver bubble of the *Breitling Orbiter 3* balloon feels absolutely motionless. Only our instruments tell us we are moving: 85 miles an hour. Yesterday Brian and I climbed out the hatch. As he fixed a problem with the burners, I used a fire ax to break off ten-foot-long icicles that had formed on both sides of the capsule, watching them tumble and turn as they fell toward the impossibly empty sands of Mali below. After closing the hatch, we repressurized the capsule, fired our burners, and climbed back to our cruising altitude of 23,000 feet. Now, sitting in the cockpit in front of our navigation instruments, we smiled at each other. After flying southwest for three days, we have reached the 25th parallel and entered the jet stream at last. For the first time since March 1, when we took off from Switzerland, my home country, we are heading east. We can finally say that our trip around the world has started.

For me this flight is a unique opportunity to establish a friendlier relationship with our planet. Human beings always want to control nature, but to fly around the world by balloon, even using our most advanced technology, we must harmonize with nature, following the rhythm of the wind. Unlike my previous two attempts to circle the globe, this time I feel that my dream is within reach. Our Rozière balloon, a combination hot air and helium design, is flying well and is using less propane fuel than expected. The engineers at Cameron Balloons, who built the envelope and capsule, have done an excellent job. And Brian Jones is the best partner I could have chosen. With a calm and flexible personality, he is also a fine technician and a very good pilot. But as I look down at the arid surface, images flash before my eyes of all the problems, all the failures, and all the tears we have gone through to reach this point.

In January 1997, when Wim Verstraeten and I made our first round-the-world attempt, our balloon had barely taken off before a massive fuel leak covered the floor of our pressurized cabin with kerosene, making us sick with vapors and forcing us to ditch in the Mediterranean Sea. On our second flight, in January 1998, Wim, Andy Elson, and I managed to reach Myanmar (Burma), but an unexplained loss of fuel during the first night and a lack of permission to fly over China put an end to that attempt. We stayed aloft longer than anyone had before, 9 days and 18 hours, but still we failed.

That flight had proved, above all, how important China was to our plans. Without permission to cross the Middle Kingdom, which stretched across so much of Asia, our chances would be slim. So in August 1998 I flew to Beijing with three other members of the team to persuade Chinese officials and obtained overflight permission two months later.

By the end of November the balloon was ready to fly. But then the global weather patterns turned bad, Iraq was being bombed again, and a British balloon drifted over forbidden areas of China, prompting the Chinese to withdraw permission for our flight as well. The season for round-the-world ballooning, which takes advantage of winter's more constant jet stream, was almost over by the time Swiss diplomats obtained a new approval for us to fly over China—but south of the 26th parallel to avoid sensitive or unsafe areas. That promised to be a difficult feat, since no weather pattern could guarantee such a trajectory. Nevertheless, on March 1 our meteorologists, Pierre Eckert and Luc Trullemans, gave us a green light to launch.

That morning at the Swiss village of Château-d'Oex, when Brian and I climbed into the capsule, the wind began to buffet the balloon and rattle our 32 propane fuel tanks. Brian looked a bit pale, but I was fatalistic. There was no going back. The uproar of the thousands of spectators drowned out the voices on our radio, and a burst of wind shot us upward. The last line tethering us to the ground had been cut.

We knew the first 24 hours would be crucial. In many previous round-the-world attempts, problems had appeared quickly. I could also not forget the story of my grandfather Auguste Piccard, when he took off on his first flight into the stratosphere in 1931. A whistling noise showed him there was a leak in the wall of the cabin. He finally managed to plug the leak with hemp and Vaseline, but later he found that he was unable to descend because of a release-valve cord that had become tangled. He had to wait for the night to cool his balloon in order to get back to Earth.

For Brian and me, crossing the Alps was slow but wonderful. We had a spectacular view of the Matterhorn and Mont Blanc. That evening, with the sun setting over the Côte d'Azur, we enjoyed a meal of emu steaks, rice, and vegetables, reheated in plastic bags in the kettle.

The following afternoon we passed Almería, Spain, where Colin Prescot and Andy Elson had launched *Cable & Wireless* two weeks before on their own round-the-world attempt. We had no hope of catching up with them though, since they were already over Myanmar 6,000 miles away.

Now, on the fifth day of our flight, my face is glued to the porthole as we soar over Libya. I have begun to like this desert, which 70 years ago was crossed by Antoine de Saint-Exupéry, Jean Mermoz, Henri Guillaumet, and the other pilots of the French Aéropostale whose works I read when I was a child. Suddenly the satellite fax light blinks, and a message from our control center in Geneva appears on the computer's screen.

"Our current speed of 85 miles an hour is too fast. The stream is going to take us north of the Himalaya. Let's descend to slow down and take a more southern route." Our friends in the control center have such team spirit that their messages are often written in the first person. They are all flying with us, from Alan Noble, the fight director, on down. Even though we are still four days from China, Alan is already worried. He knows we must cross the border into China at exactly the right place.

Thanks to our new altitude, we drift toward southern Egypt, over Sudan, Saudi Arabia, Yemen, Oman, then India and Bangladesh, assisted from afar by Swiss air traffic controllers, who help us gain access to forbidden areas. Not all the countries we fly over understand our goal, as shown by this radio exchange between Brian and the Burmese authorities:

"This is Rangoon control. What are your departure and landing points?"

"HB-BRA, departed from Switzerland, intention to land somewhere in Africa."

"If you're going from Switzerland to Africa, what in the hell are you doing in Burma?"

Each day, Brian and I take eight-hour shifts in the pilot's seat. While one of us flies the balloon, the other crawls beneath the covers in the bunk to sleep. We spend the rest of the time together, plotting our route on maps, discussing flight strategies, making repairs, and preparing food in the tiny kitchen area.

After nine days in the air, we are ideally positioned to enter southern China. Crossing the border in the middle of the night, we cannot see the high mountains of Yunnan Province, but we feel their effect: huge waves of wind make the balloon difficult to stabilize. The first words of the Chinese air traffic controller leave us no doubt.

"HB-BRA, remember, it is forbidden to fly north of 26 degrees."

Back at the control center in Geneva, the atmosphere is electric as they follow our progress. At one point, when we drift as close as 25 miles to the restricted area, the Chinese authorities ask us to prepare for an emergency landing. But, as if by a miracle, the wind brings us back on track. The next morning when the sky brightens, we see a China that is almost completely covered by a thick layer of clouds. During the rest of our 15-hour crossing we keep our eyes fixed on the magic numbers of our instruments: 85 miles an hour, heading 90 degrees. For 1,300 miles we have followed a straight line.

As soon as we leave China, the crew in the control center opens the first bottles of champagne. To them we have achieved the most difficult challenge of the trip. Yet we still have two oceans to cross, as well as North America.

The decision to cross the Pacific Ocean is irreversible. Ahead lies 10,000 miles of water, and the team in Geneva does not seem certain where to send us. Three days earlier we had all been shocked to hear that Colin Prescot and Andy Elson had been forced by bad weather to ditch their balloon in the Pacific off Japan. We were greatly relieved to learn that they were safely rescued—and to realized that we were now the only round-the-world balloon in the air. But the same storm that downed their balloon is still threatening.

Finally we receive a message advising us to give up on the northern route and to let ourselves be pushed south toward the Equator, where the computer models predict a jet stream will form in three or four days. We don't know what to expect. No one has ever flown a balloon so far south across the Pacific.

"We have no choice," I say to Brian.

That afternoon, as we fly past the Mariana Trench, the deepest spot on the planet, I think of my father, Jacques, who 39 years ago rode his bathyscaph to a depth of 35,800 feet. Considering my grandfather's exploration of the stratosphere and my father's journeys into the ocean abysses, I have begun to dream that my own flight around the world might fulfill our family's destiny--if there is such a destiny. Thinking about such things only increases my fear of failure. And yet I realize that I must learn to let go of my anxiety, to have confidence in life as I tried to have in the wind.

All around us the clouds seem alive. Every morning small cumulus clouds appear next to the balloon, growing little by little until they become fearsome cumulonimbus storms, able to tear the fragile skin of our balloon in their turbulence. As if guided by an invisible hand, we weave among the thunderclouds, which dissolve every night in the coolness of glorious sunsets.

When our speed drops to 25 miles an hour, we become very concerned, since we have covered less than 3,000 miles of ocean. We are flying so close to the Equator that the aluminum coating of the balloon over our heads blocks communication between the antenna on our capsule and the satellite directly above. We lose our fax and telephone links with our team.

"Brian, I have to tell you, I'm a little frightened," I say.

"I'm really pleased to hear you say that," Brian replies, "because I'm really scared."

This immense expanse of ocean has become a mirror in front of which it is impossible to fool myself. I feel naked with my emotions, my fears, and my hopes. We'd like to be farther on in our flight, but all we can do is accept being where we are, drifting in a lazy wind over the biggest ocean on the globe.

After six days of flight over the Pacific, the optimism of our meteorologists is proved right and we enter a powerful jet stream. Now, at 33,000 feet, we are delighted to race toward Mexico at 115 miles an hour. The typical cirrus clouds of the jet stream accompany us, their ice crystals glistening in the bright sunlight. But the euphoria lasts only 24 hours. At this altitude the outside temperature is minus 58°F, our burners use a lot more propane, and our cabin heater becomes less efficient. The water reserves inside the capsule have turned to ice.

Cold and exhausted, Brian and I begin to pant in the over-dry air of the cabin. Worse, we watch, powerless, as our speed drops: Somehow, we have ejected out of the jet stream over Mexico and are flying the wrong way, southeast towards Venezuela.

Wearing oxygen masks, Brian and I take turns sleeping as much as we can to regain strength. Completely out of breath, I phone my father and my wife with tears in my voice. My dream is falling apart, I tell them. So close to our goal! I decide to risk everything. We will fly as high as the balloon can take us, no matter how much propane it takes, to try to get into a jet stream that Luc and Pierre have managed to locate. According to them, the whole flight depends on it. At 35,000 feet my eyes are fixed on the instruments, and I can barely believe what I see: Degree by degree, our flight curves northeast. A bit later Brian notices that our speed is dramatically increasing. After flying over Jamaica, we are back on track.

On March 18 we have only four fuel tanks left out of 32, barely enough to cross the Atlantic. But there is no way we are going to stop our flight in the Caribbean. I remind Brian of what Dick Rutan, who flew non-stop around the world in an airplane, once wrote me: "The only way to fail is to quit." By the next day we are halfway across the ocean, flying at 105 miles an hour in the middle of a jet stream.

We cross the coast of Africa during the night, and when the sun rises on March 20, we are just a few hours away from Mauritania. These are the longest hours of my life. Western Sahara stretches in front of my eyes. I am happy to see the red sand desert again.

At 9:54 A.M. GREENWICH MEAN TIME Brian and I look at our maps incredulously: After having flown 26,050 miles, we have reached the finish line at 9°27′ west longitude, where we first headed east. We clasp hands and give each other a hug. We have achieved the craziest of our crazy dreams, the first nonstop flight around the world in a balloon. In Geneva our control center team is flooded in champagne in front of cameras from all over the world. But for us, nothing has changed. We are above the same desert we left from, and we have yet to find a suitable place to land. The fuel has held out, so, for the thrill of it as much as for a less remote landing, we fly another 2,380 miles, at speeds exceeding 130 miles an hour, reaching Egypt.

During the last night, I savor once more the intimate relationship we have established with our planet. Shivering in the pilot's seat, I have the feeling I have left the capsule to fly under the stars that have swallowed our balloon. I feel so privileged that I want to enjoy every second of the air world. During our three weeks of flight, protected by our high-tech cocoon, we have flown over millions of people suffering on this Earth, which we were looking at with such admiration. Why are we so lucky? At this moment it occurs to me that we could use the largest portion of the Budweiser Cup million-dollar prize to create a humanitarian foundation, the Winds of Hope, to promote respect for man and nature.

Very shortly after daybreak on March 21, after 19 days, 21 hours, and 47 minutes in the air, *Breitling Orbiter 3* will land in the Egyptian sand. Brian and I will be lifted away from the desert by helicopter, and we will immediately need to find words to satisfy the public's curiosity. But right now, muffled in my down jacket, I let the cold bite of the night remind me that I have not yet landed, that I am still living one of the most beautiful moments of my life. The only way I can make this instant last will be to share it with others. We have succeeded thanks to the winds of providence. May the winds of hope keep blowing around the world.

The First Women's Transcontinental Air Derby
Evelyn Trout

It all began with the Wright Brothers and Curtiss. Then came the OX5 Jennies, which were produced to train pilots to go overseas to fight in WWI. After the war, the Jennies were sold for approximately $500 each. That was the beginning of the barnstorming days that gave farmers a chance to see, and have a ride in, an airplane. Not only did the farmer's fields make good landing strips for the pilots to set down in, but also they could accommodate the large gatherings of sight seekers.

This began the age when the failures of planes and pilots topped headlines in the papers. It was a great step forward when women started flying—even though most people thought that *anyone* who took to the air was crazy or mentally "off their rocker." In 1927, Charles Lindbergh made his historic Atlantic flight, which alleviated the apprehension in most people's minds about flying. Still, when a new event happened, such as keeping a plane aloft for a long time, it created HEADLINES in the papers. The science of flying advanced as pilots attempted to go ever higher, faster and farther than the most recent record.

Cliff Henderson was a dreamer of ideas, mostly in this business of aviation. Cliff and his brother were business promoters in Los Angeles until Cliff turned to promoting aviation. In the summer of 1928, a year after Lindbergh's famous flight, Cliff made a deal with the owners of Mines Field, (now LAX). On the north side of the field he put up bleachers and staged a large air show in which Lindbergh was the leader of the "Army Musketeers" This was the main event, and it brought hundreds of people to see the show. This display was a great advancement in educating people about flying.

At this time, flyers were very interested in setting world records. I, like everyone else, was captivated by the aerial aerobatics. It was then that I became interested in seeking to break records. This show is where I first met Lindbergh and, I believe, Amelia Earhart. In my first exposure to aviation, I witnessed many accidents as well as records broken. Pilots were very busy trying to better the last recorded record.

About this time, Cliff Henderson had another dream. He had a vision of the First Women's Transcontinental Derby. A race that began in Santa Monica and ended at the Cleveland Air Show. This would be a GREAT advertisement for the upcoming weeklong show in Cleveland, Ohio. Cliff contacted many aircraft company VIPs, Lee Cronk, President of the Exchange Clubs, Mrs. Ulysses Grant McQueen, founder of the Women's Aeronautic Association of Beverly Hills, and many others in the Los Angeles area who shared in this new aviation dream. While it was officially named The First Women's Transcontinental Air Derby, Will Rogers called it "The Powder Puff Derby."

Girl pilots from all over wanted to fly in this derby. There were approximately 50 to 75 women coming to the Santa Monica Airport with hopes of borrowing, renting, or acquiring an airplane with which to enter the derby. Because of the cost there were very few of us who owned a plane. Prior to the beginning of the race, we enjoyed meeting one another and milling around between the Santa Monica Airport and Margaret Perry's airport a short distance away. The date for takeoff was August 18, 1929, and we were to arrive in Cleveland on August 24, the start of the Cleveland Air Show.

The early morning of August 18 found me full of excitement. I rushed to the airport to see my 100HP Golden Eagle Chief, which had been delivered about midnight the night before. It was so beautiful. I am sure it was just waiting for us to hurry there and admire it. After some loving pats, we pushed it over to the compass rose to start work. The compass in my plane looked "crazy." Someone had bent a piece of iron and mounted it, with the compass, onto the instrument panel. To correct the problem, the metal mounting bracket was soon replaced with a good piece of wood. The compass was compensated, and the plane was pushed back to the takeoff position. Nineteen planes took off on the first day. May Hazlip entered the derby on the following day with the written OK from the racing pilots for her to late start.

My family and friends were there to bid me farewell. Of course, all of the entrants were nervously waiting to be flagged off. Finally the race was on, and I was the fourth pilot to take off. As soon as I was airborne, I looked for places to set down in the event the engine cut off. Then I glanced at the instrument panel and found the engine had NO oil pressure! As I did not know what might happen, I turned to fly around Los Angeles instead of across it. About half way to San Bernadino, my engine oil pressure gauge began to work. An air bubble must have caused the trouble. We all landed in San Bernadino in good shape. Eventually, the gasoline truck drove around and filled the gasoline tanks on the aircraft. When it was my turn, I watched in disbelief as my two wing tanks were filled to overflowing.

The banquet scheduled that night was perfect, and the food delicious. After the girls were fed and happy, Pancho came around with a paper to change the course. Exhausted from the events of the day I desperately wanted to get some sleep, so I left them to decide the course for the next day. Thea and I were called late and were forced to change our course to Yuma via checking in over Imperial Airport. I bettered Phoebe's time to Imperial Airport by eight minutes. We would be stopping in Yuma to refuel our aircraft. My chief was FAST! However five miles this side of Yuma, I ran out of gas, I was flying very low when the engine cut off. I saw an area over in Mexico that looked like a harrowed field, and I turned for that landing spot. When I was over the area, I saw that it was a plowed field with very wide and deep furrows. I was too low to turn, and my small wheels quickly caught the furrow even though I stalled as much as possible. Over we went on our back. My damaged Chief had to be hauled into Yuma. After three days of work, I felt as though I could make Cleveland. The Chief purred along fine until I developed a dead stick 70 miles west of Cincinnati, Ohio. I had to slip into a very small field and then ground loop before running into a wire fence. A fence post tore the fabric on the right aileron. Luckily I was able to patch it with tin from an old can and bailing wire while a mechanic installed a new ignition switch. Only this 100HP engine could get us out of that small field. It was a not long before I was flying over Columbus. The other girls were already taking off after refueling for the final leg of the trip to Cleveland. After a quick refueling, I was back up in the air.

Lousie Thaden won first place in the large class planes, Gladys O'Donnell came in second, and Amelia Earhart third. Phoebe Omlie won for the small class planes, Edith Foltz was second, and Chubby Miller third.

During the race, there were a number of strange mishaps, including the death of Marvel Crosson. It was rumored that sabotage was a factor while the planes were parked at San Bernadino, CA. No one could determine what all was damaged on the aircraft. It will always remain a mystery. However, the morning we left San Bernadino, many strange things happened to several of the planes. People were seen the previous night wandering suspiciously around the planes. If the girls had seen someone tampering with another aircraft, they said nothing about it. Even today, I would like to think the girls knew nothing of the incident. Soon, Thea Rasche was forced down due to dirt in her gasoline tank. Claire Fahy was forced down as well with a broken flying wire, and she found acid on others. I ran out of gas five miles west of Yuma. Amelia nosed over as she was setting down in Yuma because of a bump on the outer part of the runway. She had to have a prop specially sent over that day. Marvel Crossen was heading to Wellton, Arizona, between Yuma and Phoenix. Sadly, Marvel was killed when she crashed into a mesquite jungle. Margaret Perry was hospitalized in St. Louise with typhoid fever. My troubles were mounting as my ignition switch gave out 70 miles west of Cincinnati. Pancho hit a Cadillac that nosed too far onto the landing strip. She damaged both her Travelair plane as well as the Cadillac. Because of the extensive damage to the Travelair, she was out of the race.

Even with the rumored sabotage, this was the first time women (or men) had participated in such a long race and finished with so few casualties. In those days, many men were afraid that women would take their jobs. Consequently, this race did nothing to improve this situation. They were somewhat jealous of the publicity that women received when we accomplished something as unusual or special as flying in the Transcontinental Air Derby.

This was a race that will live on forever in the history of aviation. I will always remember the excitement and emotion during those August flights and will forever cherish my memories and honor my friends that shared the skies.

Weather finished our trip home.

Jack Helm, the new distributor of the Golden Eagle Chief, came to Cleveland to see us arrive and watch the races. After the race, Jack came to me and asked, "Could I fly home with you?"

I said, "I would be very happy to have you as company and have you fly home with me." I flew us from Cleveland to East St. Louis where we spent the night. The next morning Jack asked if I would mind if he flew for a while, and I said "of course not." I climbed in the front; he climbed in the back and flew until we were about a half-hour west of St. Louis, where we ran into the blackest cloud I ever saw. NOW it was time to find a place to set down! We looked around for a landing strip and found a farm with some runway we felt would be good. We forgot about the land back east being called "gumbo." The minute our wheels touched down, the small wheels were grabbed as if we flew into a pool of glue. Our nose and left wing went up and down and around like scrambled eggs. We both shed some tears having to leave that beautiful Chief in such a mess. We thumbed a ride to the railroad, which brought us home with broken hearts knowing Mr. Bone would feel the same!

I have often wondered just what Jack did with that plane. Or did he just leave it there for the farmers? I never knew what Bone did with the factory and ships (very few), which has left me wondering all of these years since. There was a Golden Eagle Chief in Seattle, Washington. Mr. Gardener, the owner, had it for years. He would race and send the articles and pictures to me. He finally sold it to a nurse in Seattle. Since then, I have not heard about any of these ships having survived the years. Well, at least not as well as I have!

The First Women's Refueling Endurance Flight 1929
Evelyn Trout

In the spring of 1929, Louise Thaden suggested that it would be *great* if we could be the first pair to complete the very first woman's refueling endurance flight. I was thrilled at the thought of doing this, but when I suggested it to my boss, Mr. R.O. Bone, he almost lost his temper. His answer was "NO, I have to keep you from killing yourself! Absolutely NO!" Since I loved my job with Mr. Bone, I wrote to Louise and explained how he felt and that he would not change his mind. If I went it would mean losing my job. Also, I had promised Mr. Bone that I would fly his new, beautiful Golden Eagle Chief in the upcoming Women's Transcontinental Air Derby in August. Louise understood and shortly afterward left for the east.

Several months later, a Hollywood promoter named Mr. Ulman let the word get around town that he was looking for something new to promote. His last client, the famous movie star Rudolph Valentino, had recently passed away, and he needed a challenge. He sent Mr. Jack Sherrill to see me and ask if I would consider making a refueling endurance flight. I was so eager to make that flight that I told him I would do it after I finished flying in the "Powder Puff Derby." It turned out to be a good decision. Since I'd had four mishaps in the Derby, Mr. Bone's Chief was *not* in demand—neither was my job. As it turned out, I did get to Cleveland with the rest of the Derby flyers, even though I was no longer in a position to win. I certainly held the record for the most unusual difficulties. After the derby, Bone packed everything and headed back east, where he eventually sold his business and gave up manufacturing. I did not have any control over the mishaps but still was broken-hearted when he left.

After returning home from the Derby, Jack Sherrill and I were very busy promoting various aspects of the upcoming endurance flight. Freeman Lang promised to make an airplane radio for us. Lang was well known at local movie theaters as the Master of Ceremonies for film premiers. We wanted to broadcast our activities during the flight through a radio station in Los Angeles. At the time this was a new and novel idea, and to be legal, I acquired a radio license.

The radio arrived while we were testing our plane. It was about 2 feet square and heavy! It was put into our baggage space, and then we tried to take off. The radio was so heavy that it made our plane's tail heavy. The elevator controls were not adjustable enough to take care of the weight. This was an extremely important part of our flight. After all, Freeman Lang had spent many hours building this new radio (small radios were just an idea then). I was very disappointed and felt that I had obtained a license for nothing.

When I had traveled east to Cleveland, I had asked Eleanor Smith if she would like to go on the flight with me. "Yes" she would definitely love to go. As the time for our flight grew closer, Eleanor Smith came out to Los Angeles. She traveled by train at night and plane during the day. This was the way that cross-country air travel started. Nights were too dangerous. Pilots could not see to land in the dark if the engines gave out. I met Eleanor at the airport and brought her to our home, where Mother did a *very* good job of feeding us and making our guest comfortable.

Eleanor and I drove out to the Los Angeles Municipal Airport (now Van Nuys Airport) where the plane was being worked on, and from where we would take off when we started our flight. After several days of watching and waiting for the mechanics to finish, it seemed that we were finally ready for our trial takeoff. When we were airborne, our refueling ship, an old Liberty-engine-powered Pigeon, was to meet us and refuel our plane. It did not take long for us to find out that the slipstream of the Liberty engine was too strong for us to be able to keep our plane under the Pigeon. We were blown from side to side. We had to land and have the ground crew re-rig our plane so that it could be kept under the refueling ship.

We went through this sequence many times. Attempting to fly under the Pigeon, being blown around, landing, and *more* re-rigging of our Sunbeam plane. Each time we went up, we were able to "hold" under the refueling plane a wee bit better. After several times, we thought we were stable enough to grab the bag of oil, food, papers, etc. dangling from a rope which, when pulled 25 feet down, brought with it the gasoline nozzle. We were supposed to slide the nozzle into the large tube that was connected to the gasoline tanks inside the cabin. It was my job to hold it in place, but just as I slid the nozzle into the tube—and the gasoline was turned on from above— it suddenly parted. I swallowed gasoline and spent the night inhaling medications under a tent until morning. After more re-rigging, we tried again. This time, I got all the 25 feet of the three-quarters inch rope in the plane when suddenly we parted again. I burnt my hands badly while guiding the rope out of the plane's cockpit. After three more unsuccessful trials, we were finally up in the air to stay, for the day *and* the night.

We refueled the next morning successfully and proceeded to do our chores until about 5 p.m. At our next scheduled refueling, we had just received about half a tank of gasoline when the Liberty engine went to pieces. Smoke shot into the air as black as night, and I threw the gas hose overboard. The Liberty Pigeon had to descend, and we had to find a place to set down. We circled and prayed, hoping we, and the other crew, would not get into any trouble. We had taken on enough fuel to keep us aloft until the next morning at 3 a.m. After all of our trials and troubles, we had finally established a "First Refueling Flight for Women." This was our famous first flight that lasted 42 hours and 20 minutes and took a lot of courage.

I will forever remember that first world-record flight. Sliding under the Pigeon, the near misses with tragedy, and the thrill of landing in those dark hours in order to complete the flight. I feel blessed to have had the opportunity to make the flight *and* make history.

The Last Leg Home
Dick Rutan

An eerie silence had settled in the small cockpit. I glanced toward the heavens through the small bubble canopy and into the pitch black of the night. It was brimming with stars, and a tiny sliver of the moon came into view just above the right wing tip. There it was, the moon, just as plain as it could be, but it began to swing rapidly from right to left across the night sky. How could the moon be moving? Like clockwork for the past nine nights, the moon had come up in the east and tracked methodically west across the night sky. It took hours as it crawled from horizon to horizon. Tonight, it was a different moon. It raced across the sky in a blur. In just a few seconds, it had traveled all of the way from the right, across the front, and disappeared behind to my left. How could this be? Who was moving the moon? Why would they do that? I shook my head and tried to bring some reality to my foggy senses. For over two hundred hours of sleepless, fatiguing flight, we had been crammed into the phone booth sized cockpit and had spent every moment struggling to manage this frail, spindly craft westward.

The sun would come up and set in the Pacific Ocean, South China Sea, the Indian Ocean, Africa, the Atlantic, the Gulf of Mexico, and now back into the Pacific, as we plodded westward. Now through some incredible act of providence, we were mere hours from home. The last leg. If we could keep this incredible long-range flying machine in the air for just a handful of additional hours, we would achieve our goal of being the first ever to fly around the world on one tank of gas.

I peeked through the canopy again. The moon hasn't stopped. I can't make sense of the situation. Why is it moving? What is this eerie silence? Time turned in on itself, and the gauges, levers, switches, and instruments were the only reality I could remember. Home, my car, a bed, a bathroom with a shower, a restaurant meal with friends, all of those everyday, take-for-granted occurrences, were as far removed as if in another lifetime … in another universe.

I attempt to focus on this eerie silence with only the soft sound of the air whooshing across the wings of the airplane. With only an hour or two of sleep each night, (either stretched out on the uneven floor, or via a catnap in the pilot's seat when time would allow) I was able to keep the craft going westbound, but now the moon was making me dizzy, and the situation would only allow me to cling to a partial semblance of reality. The incredibly loud, interminable, and constant level of engine noise had dulled my brain for the last week, placing me in a semi-euphoric state on the edge of consciousness.

Now the roar was gone, and the engine noise was replaced by a most pleasant, soft rustle of wind and the strange motion of the moon. I look, and there it is. The moon moves again from the right and across my face, only to disappear off to my left. Perhaps this is the end. Or is it already over? Maybe the typhoon in the Pacific had torn the craft to bits last week, or maybe the planet Venus I had seen that night off the coast of Somalia was really an enemy jet fighter that terminated our flight with extreme prejudice. No, it might have been the angry thunderstorms over central Africa that had reached out and engulfed us as we struggled to out climb them. Or could it have been that towering cumulus cloud I stumbled into that dark night in the Mid-Atlantic had swallowed us up and ended the flight? Now this. This must be what it's like to leave earth and human existence.

Should I just lay back and allow myself to surrender to the lilting soft noise of the wind and the strange motion of the moon? Give in and not fight fate one more time? Should I simply relax, let go, and enjoy this transition into whatever or wherever?

I hear a call, but is it in my head or in my headset? A far-off voice that is not at all pleasant, but making demands and asking annoying questions, trying to take me to a different place, away from my sereneness—a place of quandaries, thinking, decision making, and hard work. This voice demands solutions to insoluble problems.

I try to push the voice from my mind; silently begging it to leave me alone, to let me stay here and relax, to float away in this most pleasant temporary euphoria far away from levers, switches, and gauges. The voice in my headset is pleading, "Voyager One, this is Mission Control. Dick, this is Mike. You got any fuel pressure? Any firing?"

What *is* this message, and why should I care? This is from some long ago past from someplace in antiquity, nowhere near my current reality. But what is reality? What is this? I have not turned the airplane. I am still on course, but the moon … what is moving it? And this voice from Mike … what's happening? My body is in a sea of thick molasses, and my mind is in a strange fog. Where am I? How did I get here? My befuddled mind struggles to find answers. I will it to go back, to retrace the steps.

Oh, yes, I remember now. It was my brother's crazy idea to build an airplane and fly it around the world. The hundred-plus volunteers whom I talked into spending five years building and testing the airplane. The same volunteers who came out to Edwards Air Force Base, California, on that cold December morning to see us off. These were the people who held their breath as we used the last bit of runway to stagger into the air only to disappear over the Pacific Ocean. They were on the other end of the transglobal radio link that was keeping us in the center of equatorial tail winds and away from killer storms. They had guided us to this point. Now, we were just a few hours from home and success. They are depending on us, and I can't let them down.

The voice is suddenly familiar. It is Mike. I know him. We had flown together testing Burt's many futuristic aircraft. That was the true reality, harsh as it was, and I had to deal with it.

I try to shake the fog from my head. "Dick," I tell myself, "you are in the Voyager. You are almost home. You can't let those people down." I shake my head again, trying to clear the thick haze of fatigue. "Okay, Dick," I convince myself, "deal with one thing at a time."

I must first remedy the silence and bring back that horrific roar of the engine. It's sinking in. The engine had stopped, and the pump failed. We have to change it and get life back into the engine. *And* we have to move fast. We're almost in the water.

The moon won't leave me alone. Who is moving the moon, and why? How can this be? Then, I figure it out. No one is moving the moon–we're in a steep spiral and we're spinning into the inky black night towards the ocean. Quick! Get the stick over, kick the rudder, and stop the spiral. Okay. Okay. I inventory the sky once again through the canopy. I did it. I stopped the moon.

I find the mic button and key it. "Voyager Mission Control, this is Voyager One. Mike, we got the engines running. I got Edwards on the nose, and we'll see you at eight o'clock."

EPILOGUE

Poppa's Last First Flight
Don Shepperd

*The following is an excerpt from Don Shepperd's book
"The Wheat Ridge Chronicles"*

The old man stood in front of the airplane with his hands on his bony hips. His frame was stooped and bent. His skin, once a deep Indian-brown (he was 1/8th Cherokee Indian), was a pasty, grayish yellow. Hair that was once coal-black shot out in only a few wisps from under an old felt hat that hid his chemotherapy-induced baldness. Once 175 pounds, his weight had slipped to about 120. Dad—Poppa—was in the final ravages of cancer.

Despite his weakness, Poppa insisted that he accompany me from Aransas County Airport, near Rockport, Texas, to David Wayne Hooks Memorial Airport, just north of Houston. Knowing that Poppa did not have much time to live, I scheduled a business trip to Texas. I was the national sales manager of the light aircraft division of Grumman American Aviation Corporation in Cleveland, Ohio, and was responsible for selling airplanes and establishing airport dealerships. I flew a light, two-seat airplane all the way from Cleveland to Texas, fighting bad weather and icing all the way, to conduct business and see Poppa. The weather cleared, and it was a sunny, warm south Texas day, so I decided to make the two-hour flight north in the little puddle-jumper to visit a prospective dealer.

"Poppa," I said. "I think this is a really bad idea. You are weak, and this is going to be a two-hour flight each way. The winds are light today, so it shouldn't be rough, but this little puddle-jumper airplane is still pretty uncomfortable on long flights. Let me take you home, and I'll be back by mid-afternoon."

"No, Son. I want to do this. You're flying over my old country here. If I don't beat this stuff, this may be the last time I get to fly with you. So, let's go."

Poppa had flown with me on several occasions. He had been interested in aviation ever since an old "Jenny" aircraft crashed while attempting a landing in the field behind his house just after World War I. He had wanted to be a pilot ever since and enlisted in the Army Air Corps in 1929 only to find out the recruiter had failed to mention that he needed passing scores on the pilot tests, "AND" (not, "OR") a college degree.

Poppa became a crew chief (airplane mechanic) at what is now Randolph Air Force Base, Texas, on the outskirts of San Antonio. Randolph was, and still is, a major pilot training base, and Poppa bummed rides in the backseat with pilots on test flights and weekend cross-country flights. I still have the pictures he took from the backseat of the old open-cockpit training planes. He related that on weekends, the young instructor pilots would pack him and another crew chief (along with their tools) in the backseats of two airplanes and head for Mexico, where they would land in an open field near a town. Then the pilots would go to town and drink beer, while he and his cohort were left on guard duty to prevent the cows from eating the fabric on the airplanes. After the pilots returned, they all flew home at night under moonlit skies. It was great fun for a young man with only a high school education during the Great Depression, and it introduced my father to the world of flight.

Even after Poppa realized he could not be a military pilot, he dreamed of "soloing" (flying alone) in an airplane. After several flights in the back seat as a mechanic, he considered stealing an airplane from the flightline at Randolph. Then he thought about the certain court martial, and the several years of hard labor that would follow, and reconsidered.

Poppa's legacy and love of flight was passed on to me. During and after World War II and Korea, most dinnertime conversations at our home were filled with talk of military exploits and aviation. As the nation entered the "Jet Age," we took every opportunity to read about aerial events, attend air shows, and park by commercial airports to watch the airplanes. We made model airplanes together;

the old kind that were carved from balsa wood blocks—the kind with the decals that had to be soaked off under water and that taught young boys to say, "SHIT!" when the decals crumpled up into unusable balls. My bedroom ceiling was covered with models hanging from strings: DC-3s, 4s and 6s, Corsairs, F-80s, P-51 Mustangs, F-84s and the "new" F-86. Because Poppa passed his interest in aviation on to me, I have wanted to be a pilot from the time I was five years old.

I learned that it would be possible to "solo" (fly alone) upon reaching the age of 14, and I would be able to obtain a pilot's license two years later when I turned 16. Shortly after my fourteenth birthday, I took a bus to Combs Aviation at Stapleton Field, the commercial airport serving Denver, to inquire about the cost of becoming a pilot. The kind, old pilot behind the desk took the time to carefully lay out the cost of flight instruction. The figures were staggering. He showed a plan to me that explained what I could do to offset some of the cost by working as a "lineboy" performing duties such as assisting with the refueling, maintenance, and towing of airplanes. I eagerly took the plan home to my father.

"Son," my father started off sadly. "I'm impressed that you went over on your own to investigate this. I know how much you want to fly. I can see it in your eyes and have heard it in your voice as I told flying stories and we discussed aviation during the wars ... but, Son, there's no way ... no way. It's all we can do to make ends meet on what we've got. There's no way I can take you to Stapleton Field on a regular basis and afford flying lessons for you, even if you do some lineboy work to help with the cost. It's just not doable, Son. We don't have the money. You'll have to wait until you can afford it on your own."

I could sense Poppa's disappointment. There was even a little shame in his voice. I could tell it hurt him to admit he could not afford this for his son, something that he had dreamed of doing himself when he was young. But, when I saw those staggering figures given to me by the old pilot from Combs Aviation: the cost of dual flying instruction, the cost of ground instruction, the cost of aircraft rental, and the total hours required, I knew the answer before I asked. I would have to become a pilot on my own.

Since my father (lacking a college education) was not able to enter military pilot training, he participated vicariously with great pride as I finally received an appointment to the Air Force Academy, and after graduation, entered training in Arizona to become a pilot. I'm not sure who was prouder, Poppa or I, when he pinned the silver wings on my chest at Williams Air Force Base, Arizona, in 1963. He visited several times after I moved across town to enter fighter training at Luke Air Force Base. There the sleek, new (at that time) supersonic F-100 fighter jets were something beyond his wildest dreams. I saw envy in his eyes as I sat in the cockpit and instructed him as to the functions of each switch. I told him how we conducted bombing and gunnery attacks. Then, I explained how we used the "afterburner" to inject raw fuel into the exhaust plume in the tailpipe to be reignited for extra thrust as we fought aerial "dog-fights" against each other on training missions. I even took him to the Luke Fighter Pilot Stag Bar, which was a notorious Friday night hangout for fighter pilots. Those were the days before the deglamorization of alcohol, and the characters in the bar resembled those from the famous Star Wars bar scenes. He watched young officers fueling their newly found, testosterone-laden, fighter pilot egos with storytelling, goldfish-eating and beer-chugging contests– all part of the ritual of the old Air Force. Poppa was both envious and proud.

After Luke, I was assigned to a tour in Europe. While I was there, Poppa followed my aviation progress through F-100 fighters at Hahn Air Base in Germany. As a pilot, I sat nuclear alert in Germany, Italy, and Turkey and deployed for conventional gunnery training to Wheelus Air Force Base in Libya every three months. Poppa reveled in the pictures and 8mm movies I sent home that recorded the flights and sights of Europe, the Mediterranean, and North Africa. I was doing all the things that he had dreamed of doing as a kid.

After Europe, I went to Vietnam and sent Poppa pictures, letters, and tapes about my missions. I know he was with me in spirit on all my missions. I remember the first time I was hit by anti-aircraft fire. Coming home with a crippled aircraft, I thought, "Hey, Poppa, you never told me about this part."

Poppa watched me finish my preflight inspection of the little two-seater aircraft. "Quite a step down from your jets, eh?" he questioned.

"Well, certainly in speed and performance, but light airplane flying has a joy all its own," I replied. "You can really get down amongst 'em and enjoy the sights. Jump in and let's go!" The term "jump in" hardly applied to my father's movements. He was terribly wasted, and it was all he could do, with my help, to get into the airplane.

The engine jumped to life. Since the Aransas County Airport was an uncontrolled field, we taxied to the end of the runway and checked out the aircraft systems as we let the engine oil warm to takeoff temperatures. "You handle the radios," I instructed. "I'll tell you what to say."

We turned the aircraft in a circle on the ground before takeoff, looking into the sky for other airplanes. "Yankee 61 Kilo, taking off to the east at Aransas County," Poppa repeated into the microphone to inform other aircraft that might be operating in the airport traffic pattern.

"Roger, Baron 41 Alpha, entering downwind for landing, Aransas County," came a reply. We looked to the north and saw the twin-engine aircraft turning onto the downwind leg. We checked the final approach for traffic one last time, pulled onto the runway, pushed the throttle forward, and were on our way.

"Put your feet on the rudders and your hands on the yoke and follow through with me," I instructed Poppa. Although he had flown many times, he had never received any formal instruction. He understood the principles of flight, but had never actually practiced the basics. I released the brakes and continued the instruction, "OK, now you can feel the torque from the engine taking hold. We need right rudder and a little brake here at first to keep the nose pointed straight down the runway centerline. A little more rudder now … OK, here at about 30 knots the rudder is totally effective and you don't need any brakes. Now feel the nose get light as we gain speed. OK, here we are at about 60 knots. We'll start to ease in a little backpressure on the yoke, and voila! Here we are airborne at about 70. Now we'll continue our climb at 80 knots." I raised the flaps, and we made a 45-degree turn to exit the airport traffic pattern—standard procedure for uncontrolled airports throughout the U.S.—then we turned north-northeast toward the Houston area.

"OK, Poppa, we'll level off here at about 15 hundred feet. You've got the airplane. Just hold this course until you get used to the controls." Poppa was a natural. I showed him how the trim worked, and he had no problem holding altitude and course. We practiced a few turns, and when he realized *he* was in control, not the airplane, a smile came to his face. "OK, let me have the airplane, and let's go down low-level so you can really see things, Poppa."

We descended to about 200 feet and I told Poppa to keep his eyes peeled for radio and TV towers as well as power lines, all of which are common in Texas. The weather was perfect; the air smooth as glass. The south Texas coastal landscape is very flat and sparsely populated and we began to see cattle and wild game.

"I've never seen so many deer!" exclaimed Poppa.

"Well, you've never had a God's-eye view from 200 feet," I yelled back over the engine noise. "Look over there—a herd of javelina!" I went into a hard, steep bank around the herd of scurrying wild pigs, putting them in view out my father's side of the airplane.

Really getting into it, he said, "Wow! This is something!" I dipped down just a few feet above the ground, watching carefully for trees and telephone wires as we chased the pigs. Deer also scampered in all directions. Poppa was right; I had never seen so many deer as I did this day.

"Perhaps the Lord designed this day just for us," I thought, as I glanced at the sick old man, now totally absorbed in the moment. "Let me take you up and I'll show you how we made bombing runs in Vietnam." We climbed slowly up to about 2,500 feet. "Now, let's say that water tank off to the left is our target," I shouted. "Here's how we would do it." I pulled the nose up and reduced the throttle to dissipate airspeed, then rolled sharply left and pulled down into a 45-degree dive, placing the tank squarely in the middle of the windscreen. I tracked the target for about four seconds. The windmilling propeller, with the engine at idle, kept the airspeed from building above the red line. I shouted, "PICKLE!" (Meaning, I had hit the "pickle button" on the stick—the button that sent an electrical impulse, releasing the bombs.) Then, unlike Vietnam, I pulled carefully back on the yoke to keep from over-stressing the wings of the light aircraft. "Now in Vietnam, we would pull really hard—6 Gs!—and turn quickly to make it hard for gunners," I shouted above the engine noise. "And, we'd do it from a lot higher altitude and 500 knots instead of 120."

"SHIT HOT!" shouted Poppa, and he laughed heartily. It was an expression he had heard in the fighter pilot bars. It was used often and loosely translated meant, "THAT'S GOOD," or, "WELL DONE," in polite vernacular.

"Have you had enough excitement?" I questioned, hoping I had not made Poppa airsick.

"Can we do a roll?" he asked.

I looked at him quizzically. "Well, this airplane is not certified for aerobatics, but yes, I can do it without overstressing the wings. But we have to be very careful! Hold on and follow me through." I banked the aircraft left, letting the nose down, and dove to pick up airspeed. Approaching the redline on the airspeed indicator, I very carefully began to raise the nose so as not to overstress the wings. As the nose approached 30 degrees nose-up, I carefully moved the yoke left, coordinating with the left rudder and pushed forward a little to remain slightly light in the seat. All the while, making certain the nose did not fall too far below the horizon. To finish the roll, I brought the nose up smoothly to the horizon.

"DOUBLE SHIT HOT!!!" yelled Poppa. "Can we do a loop?"

"NOPE! DOUBLE NOPE!!!" I replied. "That's asking for real trouble in this airplane. Actually, you can do it, but it's dangerous, especially when we're heavy with two people and fuel, like now. One little mistake and you can pull the tail off. We're not going to press our luck. Don't ever let anyone try a loop with you unless the airplane is certified for it."

"I doubt there's much danger of that now." Suddenly, he looked sad, and I had a mad desire to put the airplane into a loop—one last loop for Poppa! Needless to say, my flying judgment, built up over many years of taking calculated risks, would not let me do it.

I could see he was tired, so we climbed back up to 3,500 feet. I tuned-in and homed-on the Wharton non-directional beacon. The visibility was unlimited, and we could already see the outskirts of

Houston. In order for him to see better, I continued climbing to 9,500 feet and pointed out Texas City and Galveston, both southeast of Houston in the area where he grew up.

"LOOK!" he exclaimed. "THERE'S ALVIN!!!" It was the town where he was raised. "See that railroad running northwest out of Galveston? It's the third town up towards Houston." By golly, the old guy had fighter pilot eyes and an amazing sense of orientation. I definitely came by my fighter pilot genes honestly.

"OK," I said. "I've got an appointment at David Wayne Hooks Airport, so we need to get up there first. On the way back, we'll fly over Alvin." He gave me a thumbs-up.

I coordinated passage on the radio through what was then called the Houston Terminal Control Area, while I instructed Poppa on what to do with the airplane. We descended into the pattern at David Wayne Hooks, and I took over the controls. Poppa followed me through on the controls as we landed and taxied onto the ramp.

As I cut the engine, I looked at Poppa. He was ashen and obviously very tired. I talked to the lineboy and asked him to fill the tanks and if he could give us a ride into the reception room. It was all Poppa could do to get out of the airplane. Inside, I sat him in a large, padded chair and got him a bowl of soup and some crackers from the small adjoining restaurant. As I paid for the gas, the lineboy asked, "Is that old guy OK? Doesn't look much like he should be flying."

"Yeah, he's OK," I replied. "In fact, he's … he's SHIT HOT!" The lineboy was taken aback.

"He's what?" he asked.

"He's fine," I assured the boy.

After I conducted my meeting, and we went back to the airplane and took off for home. I coordinated our way back through the Houston area talking with Houston Approach Control. We crossed Houston's old Hobby Airport and followed the highway south to Alvin, Poppa's hometown. This time we circled Alvin at about 1,500 feet.

"Boy! It's grown!" Poppa shouted. "I can see where our old house was. Looks like it's a shopping center now. I can see where Uncle Dick lived. Right down there is where that old Jenny crashed-

-covered with houses. Our school's gone ... long gone. There's the cemetery where Mama and Papa are buried."

I was suddenly sad that I hadn't known my grandparents, Mama and Papa. Papa died when Dad was six years old, and Mama died a few months after I was born. I never met either of them. After Papa's death, my father and his brothers helped support the family by hunting and fishing down in the very fields that we were circling. Poppa had never seen any of this from the air. I think he would have circled until we ran out of gas.

"OK, let's go down over Galveston and then back to Aransas," I offered. "We'll fly low all the way down the coastline home." Poppa smiled. It was obvious he would have been a good fighter pilot—he loved to fly close to the ground.

We circled over Galveston. Poppa took one last glance back at Alvin. I think he knew it was the last time he would see it. We descended lower and flew at about 300 feet right down the beaches of Galveston Island (25 years ago, the beaches were virtually deserted). Soon, we passed the end of Galveston Island and approached the Matagorda Peninsula.

"Poppa, I need to rest," I lied. "I want you to fly us home. I'm going to catch some shut-eye. Now, just follow the coastline and stay at about this altitude. Watch for other airplanes! There shouldn't be any towers out here just off the shoreline. So, stay about 100 yards offshore. Watch for birds. Oh, and another thing—watch the fuel! When it gets to here (I pointed to the gauge), switch tanks to keep us balanced. After we get past this peninsula, we come up on Matagorda Island." I pointed to the map. "If you get to Mustang Island, or Corpus, we've gone too far. So, wake me up." He nodded and took the map.

My plan was to pretend to sleep, while letting him think he was flying the airplane. I intended to put my head back, close my eyes, and peep out imperceptibly through the slits to keep him honest and us safe. I slumped down in the seat and put my head back on the headrest. Poppa followed my instructions. He held altitude at about 300 feet and began to make turns to follow the shoreline. He made wide diversions around flocks of birds. The next thing I knew, he hit me on the shoulder.

"Wake up!" he said. "We're coming up on the Aransas area."

"Holy shit!" I exclaimed. I had been asleep for over 30 minutes! My heart skipped a beat as I glanced at the fuel gauge.

"I switched fuel tanks," he said, "just like you told me. There's the airport over that way," he pointed. I shook my head. Not only had the old man done as I instructed, but he had kept the fuel balanced and found the airport.

We announced our presence on the airport Unicom frequency and entered the pattern for landing. "Can we shoot a couple of touch-and-goes ... and let me do 'em?" Poppa asked.

"You really want to do some touch-and-goes? Aren't you exhausted?" I queried. He nodded. I told him to follow me through in the first one to give him the picture. "Now look, takeoffs and flying are easy. Landing is the tough part." I set us up on final approach. "Now, this is the sight picture you want. Hold about 80 knots and keep the power on all the way down until you get very close to the ground." I had him follow me through the first landing.

On the second landing I gave the airplane to him. "Add some power. You're getting slow ... let the nose down ... OK, now ease the power off and bring the nose up slightly ... WHOOPS!" I took the controls. "You ballooned. With the power off, you'll smash the nose and the prop." I added power and let the aircraft settle onto the runway. "Let's try again." We added power and he made the takeoff.

The second landing was better, but I still had to take the controls. "One more," I said. "We've got gas for one more." I talked him around the pattern, and he settled into the third and final approach. "OK, we're a little steep. Power back. OK, power back in ... looks good ... looks good ... now, ease the power off and bring the nose back slightly." It was one of those landings where the instructor pilot "should" take the controls. I wanted to grab the controls, but I also wanted to let him make the landing. I gritted my teeth and started to grab the yoke but resisted at the last moment. We hit hard and bounced. "Power in!" I instructed. He put in a little power, and we settled back onto the runway. "Not real pretty, but any landing you can walk away from is a good one," I joked. "And I've made worse ones myself."

We pulled into the parking space. I shut off the engine and jumped out to put chocks against the wheels and tie down the wings. He sat in the cockpit. As I finished the tie down, Poppa struggled out onto the ramp and stood in front of the airplane. He put his hands on his hips and gazed a long time without saying a word, as if burning the moment into his memory. It was his last "first" flight. He had conquered the air. In his own mind he was a pilot!

We went back to Mother and Poppa's mobile home. Although he was totally exhausted, we sat up late discussing the flight and what he had seen for the first time from the air. "I think this was the best day of my life," he said, just before he dozed off in his chair.

Poppa died of cancer on July 3, 1974. At the funeral home, I asked for some time alone with him. Mother and the others left the room. I told him how much I loved him and how I would miss him. I told him I would look after Mother. I thanked him for being a good dad and for everything he had done for me. I thanked him for introducing me to the world of flight. I said I hoped he was proud of me and that I had something for him. I reached into my suit pocket and pulled out my civilian flight logbook. I tore out a page and on it I wrote: "Harold Donald Shepperd—CLEARED FOR SOLO." I signed the page and put my instructor number under the signature. I folded the page and put it in his suit pocket. Poppa was now officially a pilot—forever.